First World War
and Army of Occupation
War Diary
France, Belgium and Germany

41 DIVISION
Divisional Troops
Duke of Cambridge's Own (Middlesex Regiment)
19th Battalion Pioneers
15 May 1916 - 31 October 1919

WO95/2627/3

The Naval & Military Press Ltd
www.nmarchive.com
Published in association with The National Archives

Published by

The Naval & Military Press Ltd

Unit 10 Ridgewood Industrial Park,

Uckfield, East Sussex,

TN22 5QE England

Tel: +44 (0) 1825 749494

www.naval-military-press.com

www.nmarchive.com

This diary has been reprinted in facsimile from the original. Any imperfections are inevitably reproduced and the quality may fall short of modern type and cartographic standards.

© Crown Copyright
Images reproduced by permission of The National Archives, London, England, 2015.

Contents

Document type	Place/Title	Date From	Date To
Heading	WO95/2627/3 & 4.		
Heading	19th Bn Middx Regt (Pioneers) May 1916-Oct 1917 Mar 1918-1919 Oct To Rhine Garison Troops Italy 1917 Nov-1918 Feb		
Heading	War Diary. 19th (S) Bttn. Middx Rgt (Pioneers.) 14th To 31st. May 1916.		
War Diary	Grand Rebecque Farm	15/05/1916	15/05/1916
War Diary	Les Twis Tileuls	15/05/1916	15/05/1916
War Diary	Grand Rebecque Farm	16/05/1916	16/05/1916
War Diary	Les Twis Tilleuls	16/05/1916	16/05/1916
War Diary	Grand Rebecque Farm	17/05/1916	17/05/1916
War Diary	Vicinity Of Le Tonquet Stn	17/05/1916	17/05/1916
War Diary	Les Twis Tilleuls	17/05/1916	17/05/1916
War Diary	Vicinity Of Le Tonquet Stn	18/05/1916	18/05/1916
War Diary	Grand Rebecque Farm	18/05/1916	18/05/1916
War Diary	Vicinity Of Le Tonquet Stn	18/05/1916	18/05/1916
War Diary	Les Twis Tilleuls	18/05/1916	18/05/1916
War Diary	Vicinity Of Le Tonquet Stn	19/05/1916	19/05/1916
War Diary	Grand Rebecque Farm	19/05/1916	19/05/1916
War Diary	Vicinity Of Le Tonquet Stn	19/05/1916	19/05/1916
War Diary	La Twis Tilleuls	19/05/1916	19/05/1916
War Diary	Vicinity Of Le Tonquet Stn	20/05/1916	20/05/1916
War Diary	Grand Rebecque Farm	20/05/1916	20/05/1916
War Diary	Le Binget	20/05/1916	20/05/1916
War Diary	Vicinity Of Le Tonquet Stn	20/05/1916	20/05/1916
War Diary	Les Twis Tilleuls	20/05/1916	20/05/1916
War Diary	Vicinity Of Le Tonquet Stn	20/05/1916	20/05/1916
War Diary	Les Twis Tilleuls	20/05/1916	20/05/1916
War Diary	Grand Rebecque Farm	21/05/1916	21/05/1916
War Diary	Les Twis Tilleuls	21/05/1916	22/05/1916
War Diary	Le Bizet	22/05/1916	22/05/1916
War Diary	Vicinity Of Le Tonquet Stn	22/05/1916	23/05/1916
War Diary	Grand Rebecque Farm	23/05/1916	23/05/1916
War Diary	Le Bizet	23/05/1916	23/05/1916
War Diary	Vicinity Of Le Tonquet Stn	23/05/1916	23/05/1916
War Diary	Les Twis Tilleuls,	23/05/1916	23/05/1916
War Diary	Ammenities	24/05/1916	24/05/1916
War Diary	Vicinity Of Le Tonquet Stn	24/05/1916	24/05/1916
War Diary	Ammenities	24/05/1916	24/05/1916
War Diary	Grand Rebecque Farm	24/05/1916	24/05/1916
War Diary	Vicinity Of Le Tonquet Stn	24/05/1916	24/05/1916
War Diary	Les Twis Tillets	24/05/1916	24/05/1916
War Diary	Le Bizet	24/05/1916	25/05/1916
War Diary	Vicinity Of Le Tonquet Stn	25/05/1916	25/05/1916
War Diary	Grand Rebecque Farm	25/05/1916	25/05/1916
War Diary	Vicinity Of Le Tonquet Stn	25/05/1916	25/05/1916
War Diary	Les Twis Tillets	25/05/1916	25/05/1916
War Diary	Vicinity Of Le Tonquet Stn	25/05/1916	25/05/1916
War Diary	Les Twis Tilleul	25/05/1916	25/05/1916
War Diary	Vicinity Of Le Tonquet Stn	26/05/1916	26/05/1916

War Diary	Les Twis Tilleul	26/05/1916	26/05/1916
War Diary	Grand Rebecque Farm	27/05/1916	27/05/1916
War Diary	Vicinity Of Le Tonquet Stn	27/05/1916	27/05/1916
War Diary	Les Tonquet Tilleul	27/05/1916	27/05/1916
War Diary	Vicinity Of Le Tonquet Stn	28/05/1916	28/05/1916
War Diary	Nieppe	27/05/1916	27/05/1916
War Diary	Vicinity Of Le Tonquet Stn	29/05/1916	29/05/1916
War Diary	Pretoria Avenue	29/05/1916	29/05/1916
War Diary	Vicinity of Le Tonquet Stn	30/05/1916	30/05/1916
War Diary	Ploegsteert Wood	30/05/1916	30/05/1916
War Diary	Ontario Avenue	30/05/1916	30/05/1916
War Diary	Winnepeg Avenue	30/05/1916	31/05/1916
War Diary	Ploegsteert	31/05/1916	31/05/1916
War Diary	Tonquet Battn	31/05/1916	31/05/1916
War Diary	Ploegsteert Wood	31/05/1916	31/05/1916
Miscellaneous	Officer Commanding 19th (S) Btn Middlesex Regt (Pioneers), B.E.F.	30/06/1916	30/06/1916
War Diary	Ontario Avenue	31/05/1916	31/05/1916
War Diary	Ontario Av Winnipeg Av	01/06/1916	01/06/1916
War Diary	Ploegsteert Wood	01/06/1916	01/06/1916
War Diary	Ontario Av Winnipeg Av	02/06/1916	02/06/1916
War Diary	Ploegsteert Wood	02/06/1916	02/06/1916
War Diary	Warnave Avenue	02/06/1916	02/06/1916
War Diary	Ploegsteert Wood	02/06/1916	02/06/1916
War Diary	Ontario Av Winnipeg Av	03/06/1916	03/06/1916
War Diary	Ploegsteert Wood	03/06/1916	03/06/1916
War Diary	Warnave Av	03/06/1916	03/06/1916
War Diary	Ploegsteert Wood	03/06/1916	03/06/1916
War Diary	Warnave Av	04/06/1916	04/06/1916
War Diary	Ontario Avenue	05/06/1916	05/06/1916
War Diary	Ploegsteert Wood	05/06/1916	05/06/1916
War Diary	Warnave Avenue	05/06/1916	05/06/1916
War Diary	Ploegsteert Wood	05/06/1916	05/06/1916
War Diary	Warnave Avenue	06/06/1916	06/06/1916
War Diary	Ontario Avenue	06/06/1916	06/06/1916
War Diary	Warnave Avenue	06/06/1916	06/06/1916
War Diary	Ploegsteert Wood	06/06/1916	06/06/1916
War Diary	Warnave Avenue	07/06/1916	07/06/1916
War Diary	Ontario Avenue	07/06/1916	07/06/1916
War Diary	Ploegsteert Wood	07/06/1916	07/06/1916
War Diary	Warnave Avenue	07/06/1916	07/06/1916
War Diary	Ploegsteert Wood	07/06/1916	07/06/1916
War Diary	Warnave Avenue	08/06/1916	08/06/1916
War Diary	Ontario Avenue	08/06/1916	08/06/1916
War Diary	Ploegsteert Wood	08/06/1916	08/06/1916
War Diary	Warnave Avenue	08/06/1916	08/06/1916
War Diary	Ploegsteert Wood	08/06/1916	08/06/1916
War Diary	Ontario Avenue	09/06/1916	09/06/1916
War Diary	Ploegsteert Wood	09/06/1916	09/06/1916
War Diary	Warnave Avenue	09/06/1916	09/06/1916
War Diary	Ploegsteert Wood	09/06/1916	09/06/1916
War Diary	Ontario & Anscroft Avenues	10/06/1916	10/06/1916
War Diary	Ploegsteert Wood	10/06/1916	10/06/1916
War Diary	Warnave Avenue	10/06/1916	10/06/1916
War Diary	Ploegsteert Wood	10/06/1916	10/06/1916
War Diary	Support Line	02/06/1916	10/06/1916

War Diary	Warnave Avenue	11/06/1916	11/06/1916
War Diary	Ploegsteert Wood	11/06/1916	11/06/1916
War Diary	Ontario Avenue Anscroft Avenue	12/06/1916	12/06/1916
War Diary	Ploegsteert Wood	12/06/1916	12/06/1916
War Diary	Warnave Avenue	12/06/1916	12/06/1916
War Diary	Ploegsteert Wood	12/06/1916	12/06/1916
War Diary	Ontario Av Anscroft Av	13/06/1916	13/06/1916
War Diary	Ploegsteert Wood	13/06/1916	13/06/1916
War Diary	Border Rd	13/06/1916	13/06/1916
War Diary	Ploegsteert Wood	13/06/1916	13/06/1916
War Diary	Ontario & Anscroft Av	14/06/1916	15/06/1916
War Diary	Lowndes Av	15/06/1916	15/06/1916
War Diary	Border Avenue	15/06/1916	15/06/1916
War Diary	Ploegsteert Wood	15/06/1916	15/06/1916
War Diary	Ontario & Anscroft Av	16/06/1916	16/06/1916
War Diary	Ploegsteert Wood	16/06/1916	16/06/1916
War Diary	Border Av	16/06/1916	16/06/1916
War Diary	Ploegsteert Wood	16/06/1916	16/06/1916
War Diary	Support Line	15/06/1916	17/06/1916
War Diary	Ontario & Anscroft Av	17/06/1916	17/06/1916
War Diary	Lowndes Lane	17/06/1916	17/06/1916
War Diary	Border Av	17/06/1916	17/06/1916
War Diary	Tilleul	17/06/1916	17/06/1916
War Diary	Ontario & Annscroft Av	18/06/1916	18/06/1916
War Diary	Ploegsteert Wood	18/06/1916	18/06/1916
War Diary	Border Av	18/06/1916	18/06/1916
War Diary	Ploegsteert Wood	18/06/1916	18/06/1916
War Diary	Support Line		
War Diary	Ontario & Annscroft Av	19/06/1916	19/06/1916
War Diary	Lowndes Lane	19/06/1916	19/06/1916
War Diary	Border Av	19/06/1916	19/06/1916
War Diary	Ploegsteert Wood	19/06/1916	19/06/1916
War Diary	Ontario & Annscroft Av	20/06/1916	20/06/1916
War Diary	Lowndes Lane	20/06/1916	20/06/1916
War Diary	Border Av	20/06/1916	20/06/1916
War Diary	Ploegsteert Wood	20/06/1916	20/06/1916
War Diary	Ontario & Annscroft Av	22/06/1916	22/06/1916
War Diary	Ploegsteert Wood	22/06/1916	22/06/1916
War Diary	Border Av	22/06/1916	22/06/1916
War Diary	Ploegsteert Wood	22/06/1916	22/06/1916
War Diary	Ontario & Annscroft Av	23/06/1916	23/06/1916
War Diary	Ploegsteert Wood	23/06/1916	23/06/1916
War Diary	Border Av	23/06/1916	23/06/1916
War Diary	Ploegsteert Wood	23/06/1916	23/06/1916
War Diary	Ontario & Annscroft Av	24/06/1916	24/06/1916
War Diary	Ploegsteert Wood	24/06/1916	24/06/1916
War Diary	Border Av	24/06/1916	24/06/1916
War Diary	Ploegsteert Wood	24/06/1916	24/06/1916
War Diary	Support Line	18/06/1916	24/06/1916
War Diary	Ontario & Annscroft Av	25/06/1916	25/06/1916
War Diary	Ploegsteert Wood	25/06/1916	25/06/1916
War Diary	Border Avenue	25/06/1916	25/06/1916
War Diary	Ploegsteert Wood	25/06/1916	25/06/1916
War Diary	Oosthove Farm	25/06/1916	25/06/1916
War Diary	Ontario & Annscroft Av	26/06/1916	26/06/1916
War Diary	Ploegsteert Wood	26/06/1916	26/06/1916

War Diary	Border Avenue	26/06/1916	26/06/1916
War Diary	Ploegsteert Wood	26/06/1916	26/06/1916
War Diary	Oosthove Farm	26/06/1916	26/06/1916
War Diary	Ontario & Annscroft Av	27/06/1916	27/06/1916
War Diary	Ploegsteert Wood	27/06/1916	27/06/1916
War Diary	Border Av	27/06/1916	27/06/1916
War Diary	Ploegsteert Wood	27/06/1916	27/06/1916
War Diary	Ontario & Annscroft Av	29/06/1916	29/06/1916
War Diary	Ploegsteert Wood	29/06/1916	29/06/1916
War Diary	Border Avenue	29/06/1916	29/06/1916
War Diary	Ploegsteert Wood	29/06/1916	29/06/1916
War Diary	Oosthoek Farm	30/06/1916	30/06/1916
Miscellaneous	O.C., 19th (P.W.P.) Bn. Middlesex Regt.	31/07/1916	31/07/1916
Miscellaneous	Officer Commanding 19th (S) B'n Middlesex Regt (Pioneers), B.E.F.	31/07/1916	31/07/1916
War Diary	Ontario & Annscroft Av	01/07/1916	01/07/1916
War Diary	Lowndes Av Hunters Av	01/07/1916	01/07/1916
War Diary	Lewisham Au	01/07/1916	01/07/1916
War Diary	Ploegsteert Wood	01/07/1916	01/07/1916
War Diary	Oosthove Farm	01/07/1916	01/07/1916
War Diary	Ontario & Annscroft Av	02/07/1916	02/07/1916
War Diary	Lowndes & Hunters Av	02/07/1916	02/07/1916
War Diary	Lewisham Au	02/07/1916	02/07/1916
War Diary	Ploegsteert Wood	02/07/1916	02/07/1916
War Diary	Ontario & Annscroft Av	03/07/1916	03/07/1916
War Diary	Lowndes Av Hunters Av	03/07/1916	03/07/1916
War Diary	Lewisham AV	03/07/1916	03/07/1916
War Diary	Ploegsteert Wood	03/07/1916	03/07/1916
War Diary	Ontario & Annscroft Av	04/07/1916	04/07/1916
War Diary	Lowndes Av Hunters Av	04/07/1916	04/07/1916
War Diary	Ploegsteert Wood	04/07/1916	04/07/1916
War Diary	Ontario & Annscroft Av	06/07/1916	06/07/1916
War Diary	Lowndes Av	06/07/1916	06/07/1916
War Diary	The Only Way	06/07/1916	06/07/1916
War Diary	Ploegsteert Wood	06/07/1916	06/07/1916
War Diary	The Only Way	07/07/1916	07/07/1916
War Diary	Ontario & Annscroft Av	07/07/1916	07/07/1916
War Diary	Lowndes Av	07/07/1916	07/07/1916
War Diary	The Only Way	07/07/1916	07/07/1916
War Diary	Ploegsteert Wd	07/07/1916	07/07/1916
War Diary	The Only Way	08/07/1916	08/07/1916
War Diary	Ontario Av N & S	08/07/1916	08/07/1916
War Diary	Lowndes Av	08/07/1916	08/07/1916
War Diary	The Only Way	08/07/1916	08/07/1916
War Diary	Ploegsteert Wood	08/07/1916	08/07/1916
War Diary	Ontario Av N & S	09/07/1916	09/07/1916
War Diary	Lowndes Av	09/07/1916	09/07/1916
War Diary	The Only Way	09/07/1916	09/07/1916
War Diary	Toronto Av	09/07/1916	09/07/1916
War Diary	Ontario Av N & S	10/07/1916	10/07/1916
War Diary	Lowndes Av	10/07/1916	10/07/1916
War Diary	The Only Way	10/07/1916	10/07/1916
War Diary	Toronto Av	10/07/1916	10/07/1916
War Diary	Ontario Av N & S	11/07/1916	11/07/1916
War Diary	Lowndes Av	11/07/1916	11/07/1916
War Diary	Only Way	11/07/1916	11/07/1916

War Diary	Toronto Av	11/07/1916	11/07/1916
War Diary	Ontario Av N & S	13/07/1916	13/07/1916
War Diary	Lowndes Av	13/07/1916	13/07/1916
War Diary	Only Way	13/07/1916	13/07/1916
War Diary	Toronto Av	13/07/1916	13/07/1916
War Diary	Ontario Av N & S	14/07/1916	14/07/1916
War Diary	Loundes Lane	14/07/1916	14/07/1916
War Diary	Only Way	14/07/1916	14/07/1916
War Diary	Toronto Av	14/07/1916	14/07/1916
War Diary	Ontario Av N & S	15/07/1916	15/07/1916
War Diary	Loundes Lane	15/07/1916	15/07/1916
War Diary	Only Way	15/07/1916	15/07/1916
War Diary	Toronto Av	15/07/1916	15/07/1916
War Diary	Ontario Av	16/07/1916	17/07/1916
War Diary	Loundes Av	17/07/1916	17/07/1916
War Diary	Only Way	17/07/1916	17/07/1916
War Diary	Toronto Av & Hill 63	17/07/1916	17/07/1916
War Diary	Only Way	18/07/1916	18/07/1916
War Diary	Ontario Av	18/07/1916	18/07/1916
War Diary	Lowndes Av	18/07/1916	18/07/1916
War Diary	Moulin Dela Rabeque Fm	18/07/1916	18/07/1916
War Diary	Only Way	18/07/1916	18/07/1916
War Diary	Toronto Av Hill 63	18/07/1916	18/07/1916
War Diary	Only Way	19/07/1916	19/07/1916
War Diary	Ontario Av	20/07/1916	20/07/1916
War Diary	Moulin De La Rabeque Farm	19/07/1916	20/07/1916
War Diary	Only Way	20/07/1916	20/07/1916
War Diary	Toronto Av Hill 63	20/07/1916	20/07/1916
War Diary	Only Way	21/07/1916	21/07/1916
War Diary	Ontario Loop Ontario Avenue	21/07/1916	21/07/1916
War Diary	Moulin Dela Rabeque Farm	22/07/1916	22/07/1916
War Diary	Only Way	21/07/1916	21/07/1916
War Diary	Toronto Av Hill 63	21/07/1916	21/07/1916
War Diary	Only Way	22/07/1916	22/07/1916
War Diary	Ontario Av & Loop	22/07/1916	22/07/1916
War Diary	Moulin De La Rabeque Farm & Lowndes Av	23/07/1916	23/07/1916
War Diary	Only Way	22/07/1916	22/07/1916
War Diary	Toronto Av Hill 63	22/07/1916	22/07/1916
War Diary	Ontario Loop & Av	23/07/1916	23/07/1916
War Diary	Only Way	23/07/1916	23/07/1916
War Diary	Toronto Av Hill 63	23/07/1916	23/07/1916
War Diary	Ontario Av & Loop	24/07/1916	24/07/1916
War Diary	M De La Rabeque Farm 4 Lowndes AU	24/07/1916	24/07/1916
War Diary	Only Way	24/07/1916	24/07/1916
War Diary	Toronto Av Hill 63	24/07/1916	24/07/1916
War Diary	Only Way	25/07/1916	25/07/1916
War Diary	Ontario Av & Loop	25/07/1916	25/07/1916
War Diary	Lowndes Av M Dela Rabeque Fm	25/07/1916	25/07/1916
War Diary	Only Way	25/07/1916	25/07/1916
War Diary	Toronto Av Hill 63	25/07/1916	25/07/1916
War Diary	Only Way	26/07/1916	26/07/1916
War Diary	Ontario Av & Loop	27/07/1916	27/07/1916
War Diary	Lowndes Av	27/07/1916	27/07/1916
War Diary	Only Way	27/07/1916	27/07/1916
War Diary	Toronto Av Hill 63	27/07/1916	27/07/1916
War Diary	Only Way	28/07/1916	28/07/1916

War Diary	Ontario Av & Loop	28/07/1916	28/07/1916
War Diary	Lowndes Av & Keepers Breastvil	28/07/1916	28/07/1916
War Diary	Only Way	28/07/1916	28/07/1916
War Diary	Toronto Av Hill 63	28/07/1916	28/07/1916
War Diary	Ontario Ave	29/07/1916	29/07/1916
War Diary	Lowndes Ave	29/07/1916	29/07/1916
War Diary	Regent St	29/07/1916	29/07/1916
War Diary	Toronto Av	29/07/1916	30/07/1916
War Diary	Ontario Ave	31/07/1916	31/07/1916
War Diary	Lowndes Ave	31/07/1916	31/07/1916
War Diary	Regent St	31/07/1916	31/07/1916
War Diary	Toronto Ave	31/07/1916	31/07/1916
War Diary	Ontario Ave	05/08/1916	05/08/1916
War Diary	Lowndes Ave	05/08/1916	05/08/1916
War Diary	Regent St	05/08/1916	05/08/1916
War Diary	Toronto Ave	05/08/1916	05/08/1916
War Diary	Ontario Ave	06/08/1916	06/08/1916
War Diary	Lowndes Ave	06/08/1916	06/08/1916
War Diary	Regent St	06/08/1916	06/08/1916
War Diary	Toronto Ave	06/08/1916	07/08/1916
War Diary	Ontario Avenue.	08/08/1916	08/08/1916
War Diary	Lowndes Ave	08/08/1916	08/08/1916
War Diary	Regent St	08/08/1916	08/08/1916
War Diary	Toronto Ave	08/08/1916	09/08/1916
War Diary	Ontario Ave	10/08/1916	10/08/1916
War Diary	Lowndes Ave	10/08/1916	10/08/1916
War Diary	Regent St	10/08/1916	10/08/1916
War Diary	Toronto Ave	10/08/1916	10/08/1916
War Diary	Ontario Ave	11/08/1916	11/08/1916
War Diary	Lowndes Ave	11/08/1916	11/08/1916
War Diary	Toronto Ave	11/08/1916	11/08/1916
War Diary	Regent St	11/08/1916	11/08/1916
War Diary	Ontario Ave	12/08/1916	12/08/1916
War Diary	Lowndes Ave	12/08/1916	12/08/1916
War Diary	Regent St	12/08/1916	12/08/1916
War Diary	Toronto Ave	12/08/1916	13/08/1916
War Diary	Ontario Ave	14/08/1916	14/08/1916
War Diary	Londres Ave	14/08/1916	14/08/1916
War Diary	Regent St	14/08/1916	14/08/1916
War Diary	Toronto Ave	14/08/1916	14/08/1916
War Diary	Oosthove	15/08/1916	16/08/1916
War Diary	Oosthove 5.36 A.3.	17/08/1916	17/08/1916
War Diary	S. 36 A.3	18/08/1916	24/08/1916
War Diary	Ailly	25/08/1916	31/08/1916
War Diary	Ailly Le Haut Clocher	01/09/1916	03/09/1916
War Diary	F.9.	04/09/1916	04/09/1916
War Diary	Milln Avenue A & D Coys	05/09/1916	05/09/1916
War Diary	Flure Ave B & C Coys.	05/09/1916	05/09/1916
War Diary	Milln Ave A & D Coys	06/09/1916	06/09/1916
War Diary	Flure Ave B & C Coys	06/09/1916	06/09/1916
War Diary	Milln Ave A & D Coys	07/09/1916	07/09/1916
War Diary	Flure Ave B & C.	07/09/1916	07/09/1916
War Diary	Milln Ave A & D Coys	08/09/1916	08/09/1916
War Diary	Flure Ave B. C Coys	08/09/1916	08/09/1916
War Diary	Milln Ave A & D Coys	09/09/1916	09/09/1916
War Diary	Flure Ave B & C Coys	09/09/1916	09/09/1916

War Diary	Milln Lure A & D Coy.	10/09/1916	10/09/1916
War Diary	Flure Luru B & C Coy	10/09/1916	10/09/1916
War Diary	Milln Luru A & D Coy	11/09/1916	11/09/1916
War Diary	Flure Luru B & C.	11/09/1916	11/09/1916
War Diary	Milln Luru A & D	12/09/1916	12/09/1916
War Diary	Flure Luru B & C.	12/09/1916	12/09/1916
War Diary	Milln Luru A & D	13/09/1916	13/09/1916
War Diary	Flure Luru B & C.	13/09/1916	13/09/1916
War Diary	Fincourt	14/09/1916	14/09/1916
War Diary	Green Dump From Quray To 17 A 3.8 A & D Coys.	15/09/1916	15/09/1916
War Diary	Montauban Rd. B & C. Coys.	15/09/1916	15/09/1916
War Diary	Green Dump Rd. A & D. Coy.	16/09/1916	16/09/1916
War Diary	Montauban Rd B & C Coys	16/09/1916	16/09/1916
War Diary	Montauban	17/09/1916	17/09/1916
War Diary	Yanhi Trench To Switch Line	18/09/1916	22/09/1916
War Diary	Faircourt Camp	22/09/1916	30/09/1916
War Diary	Cable Trench	01/10/1916	03/10/1916
War Diary	A.B.C. Acoys At Trench Luru & Fronts Alley	04/10/1916	04/10/1916
War Diary	D. Coy. On Observation Post.	04/10/1916	04/10/1916
War Diary	Trench Line & Pioneers Line A.B.C. Coys.	05/10/1916	05/10/1916
War Diary	D. Coy. Obersvation Post.	05/10/1916	05/10/1916
War Diary	Fish Alley A.	06/10/1916	06/10/1916
War Diary	Grove Alley B.	06/10/1916	06/10/1916
War Diary	Trenches Line	06/10/1916	06/10/1916
War Diary	Observation Post D.	06/10/1916	06/10/1916
War Diary	Grove Alley	07/10/1916	07/10/1916
War Diary	Trench Line & Pioneers Line	08/10/1916	09/10/1916
War Diary	Trench Line & Grove Ailly	10/10/1916	10/10/1916
War Diary	Montauban	11/10/1916	15/10/1916
War Diary	Buire	16/10/1916	17/10/1916
War Diary	Hallancourt	18/10/1916	20/10/1916
War Diary	Rouge Croix	21/10/1916	22/10/1916
War Diary	Berthen	23/10/1916	23/10/1916
War Diary	Micmac Camp	24/10/1916	31/10/1916
Miscellaneous	Officer Commanding. 19th (S) Battalion Middlesex Regt. (Pioneers.)	01/12/1916	01/12/1916
War Diary	Micmac Camp	01/11/1916	31/12/1916
Miscellaneous	Officer Commanding 19th (S) Battalion Middlesex Regt (Pioneers.)	01/02/1917	01/02/1917
War Diary	Micmac Camp	01/01/1917	31/01/1917
Miscellaneous	Officer Commanding 19th (S) Battalion Middlesex Regt. (Pioneers.)	01/03/1917	01/03/1917
War Diary	Micmac Camp	01/02/1917	28/02/1917
Heading	War Diary Of 19th. Bn Middlesex Regt. (Pioneers) For Month Of March 1917		
Miscellaneous	Officer Commanding 19th (S) Battalion Middlesex Regt. (Pioneers.)	31/03/1917	31/03/1917
War Diary	Micmac Camp	01/03/1917	30/04/1917
Miscellaneous	Officer Commanding 19th (S) Battalion Middlesex Regt. (Pioneers.)	01/06/1917	01/06/1917
War Diary	Micmac Camp	01/05/1917	31/05/1917
Miscellaneous	Officer Commanding 19th (S) Battalion Middlesex Regt. (Pioneers.)	30/06/1917	30/06/1917
War Diary	Micmac Camp	01/06/1917	06/06/1917
War Diary	G.H.Q. 2nd Lines	07/06/1917	12/06/1917
War Diary	Vierstraat	13/06/1917	30/06/1917

Type	Location	From	To
Miscellaneous	Officer Commanding 19th (S) Battalion Middlesex Regt. (Pioneers.)	01/08/1917	01/08/1917
War Diary	Berthen	01/07/1917	10/07/1917
War Diary	Millekruisse	11/07/1917	23/07/1917
War Diary	Ridge Wood	24/07/1917	30/07/1917
War Diary	Vierstraat	31/07/1917	31/07/1917
Miscellaneous	Officer Commanding 19th (S) Battalion Middlesex Regt. (Pioneers.)	31/08/1917	31/08/1917
War Diary	Vierstraat	01/08/1917	14/08/1917
War Diary	Berthen	15/08/1917	19/08/1917
War Diary	Staple	20/08/1917	20/08/1917
War Diary	Etrehem	21/08/1917	29/08/1917
War Diary	Ridge Wood	30/08/1917	25/09/1917
War Diary	L'Egerreest	26/09/1917	26/09/1917
War Diary	La Panne	27/09/1917	30/09/1917
Miscellaneous			
Miscellaneous	Officer Commanding 19th (S) Battalion Middlesex Regt. (Pioneers.)	01/11/1917	01/11/1917
Miscellaneous	Officer Commanding 19th (S) Bn. Middlesex Regt. (Pioneers)	01/10/1917	01/10/1917
War Diary	La Panne	01/10/1917	07/10/1917
War Diary	Oost Dunkerke Bains	08/10/1917	28/10/1917
War Diary	Couderkerque	29/10/1917	31/10/1917
Heading	19th Battn. The Middlesex Regiment. March 1918		
War Diary	Italy	01/03/1918	03/03/1918
War Diary	France	08/03/1918	08/03/1918
War Diary	Couturelle	09/03/1918	18/03/1918
War Diary	Arras	19/03/1918	22/03/1918
War Diary	Beugnatre	23/03/1918	24/03/1918
War Diary	Biefvillers Les-Bapaume	25/03/1918	25/03/1918
War Diary	Fonquevillers	26/03/1918	26/03/1918
War Diary	Italy	01/03/1918	02/03/1918
War Diary	France	03/03/1918	08/03/1918
War Diary	Couturelle	09/03/1918	18/03/1918
War Diary	Arras	19/03/1918	22/03/1918
War Diary	Beugnatre	23/03/1918	24/03/1918
War Diary	Biefvillers Les-Bapaume	25/03/1918	25/03/1918
War Diary	Fonquevillers	26/03/1918	26/03/1918
War Diary	Bienvillers-Au-Bois	27/03/1918	27/03/1918
War Diary	Gommecourt	28/03/1918	28/03/1918
War Diary	Ablainzevelle	29/03/1918	31/03/1918
Heading	19th Battalion The Middlesex Regiment Pioneers April 1918		
Miscellaneous	Officer Commanding 19th (S) Battalion Middlesex Regt. (Pioneers.)	01/05/1918	01/05/1918
War Diary	Ablainzevelle	01/04/1918	01/04/1918
War Diary	Halloy	02/04/1918	02/04/1918
War Diary	Beauvoir	03/04/1918	04/04/1918
War Diary	Steenvoorde	05/04/1918	08/04/1918
War Diary	La Brique	09/04/1918	12/04/1918
War Diary	Ypres	13/04/1918	25/04/1918
War Diary	Vlamertinghe	26/04/1918	30/04/1918
Miscellaneous	Officer Commanding 19th (S) Battalion Middlesex Regt. (Pioneers.)	31/05/1918	31/05/1918
War Diary	Vlamertinghe	01/05/1918	31/05/1918

Miscellaneous	Officer Commanding 19th (S) Battalion Middlesex Regt. (Pioneers.)		02/07/1918	02/07/1918
War Diary	Vlamertinghe		01/06/1918	01/06/1918
War Diary	St Jan Ter Biezen		02/06/1918	03/06/1918
War Diary	Buysscheure		04/06/1918	08/06/1918
War Diary	Eperlecques		09/06/1918	24/06/1918
War Diary	Buysscheure		25/06/1918	25/06/1918
War Diary	Zermezeele		26/06/1918	29/06/1918
War Diary	Wippenhoek		30/06/1918	30/06/1918
Miscellaneous	Officer Commanding 19th (S) B'n Middlesex Regt (Pioneers).		01/08/1918	01/08/1918
War Diary	Wippenhoek		01/07/1918	29/08/1918
War Diary	Etrehem		30/08/1918	31/08/1918
War Diary	Etrehem		01/09/1918	01/09/1918
War Diary	Hoograaf G 29 G 1.2		02/09/1918	09/09/1918
War Diary	Ouderdom G 2.2 B 12.		10/09/1918	18/09/1918
War Diary	Reninghelst G 2.2 L 6.6		19/09/1918	26/09/1918
War Diary	Brandhoek G11 V 7.6		27/09/1918	28/09/1918
War Diary	Bedford House I 26 Central		29/09/1918	30/09/1918
Miscellaneous	To D.A.G. 3rd Echelon		09/12/1918	09/12/1918
War Diary	Bedford House Ypres		01/10/1918	05/10/1918
War Diary	Hooge		06/10/1918	09/10/1918
War Diary	Klein Zillebeke		10/10/1918	13/10/1918
War Diary	Ghelowe		14/10/1918	15/10/1918
War Diary	Moorseele		16/10/1918	19/10/1918
War Diary	Bisseghem		20/10/1918	22/10/1918
War Diary	Sweyenghem		23/10/1918	26/10/1918
War Diary	Marcke		27/10/1918	31/10/1918
Miscellaneous	Officers Commanding 19th (S) Battn Middx Regt		30/11/1917	30/11/1917
War Diary	Marcke		01/11/1918	02/11/1918
War Diary	Sweveghem		03/11/1918	04/11/1918
War Diary	Ingoyghem		05/11/1918	09/11/1918
War Diary	Berchem		10/11/1918	14/11/1918
War Diary	Opbrakel		15/11/1917	18/11/1917
War Diary	Ideghem		19/11/1918	30/11/1918
Miscellaneous	Officer Commanding 19th B'n Middlesex Regt. (Pioneers.)		07/01/1919	07/01/1919
War Diary	Idegem		01/12/1918	11/12/1918
War Diary	Enghien		12/12/1918	12/12/1918
War Diary	Hal		13/12/1918	13/12/1918
War Diary	Braine L'Alleud		14/12/1918	16/12/1918
War Diary	Marbaisoux		17/12/1918	17/12/1918
War Diary	Som Breffe		18/12/1918	18/12/1918
War Diary	Dhuy		19/12/1918	19/12/1918
War Diary	Franc-Waret		20/12/1918	20/12/1918
War Diary	Bas Oha		21/12/1918	12/01/1919
War Diary	Unter-Eschbach		13/01/1919	31/01/1919
War Diary	Eschbach		01/02/1919	28/02/1919
War Diary	Unter Eschbach Germany		01/03/1919	31/03/1919
War Diary	Unter Eschbach		01/04/1919	30/04/1919
War Diary	Unter-Eschbach Germany		01/05/1919	23/05/1919
War Diary	U-Eschbach		28/05/1919	08/06/1919
War Diary	Immekeppel		09/06/1919	24/06/1919
War Diary	U-Eschbach		28/06/1919	30/06/1919
War Diary	Immekeppel		03/07/1919	03/07/1919
War Diary	Unter-Eschbach		10/03/1919	10/03/1919

War Diary	Immekeppel	13/07/1919	27/07/1919
War Diary	Unter-Eschbach	28/07/1919	29/07/1919
War Diary	Immekeppel	30/07/1919	30/08/1919
Map	19th. (S) Middlesex Regt.		
War Diary	Unter-Eschbach	01/09/1919	27/09/1919
Map	Approximate Scale		
War Diary	Wahn Barracks	02/10/1919	12/10/1919
War Diary	Bruhl	20/10/1919	31/10/1919

Mom 505/262/4 or 4.

41ST DIVISION

19TH BN MIDDX REGT
(PIONEERS)
MAY 1916-~~DEC 1918~~ OCT 1917
MAR 1918 - 1919 OCT

TO RHINE GARRISON TROOPS

ITALY 1917 NOV — 1918 FEB

// P/41

War Diary.

19th (S) Bttn. Middx Rgt
Pioneers.

14th to 31st May 1916.

Army Form C. 2118.

WAR DIARY
or
INTELLIGENCE SUMMARY.
(Erase heading not required.)

Instructions regarding War Diaries and Intelligence Summaries are contained in F. S. Regs., Part II and the Staff Manual respectively. Title pages will be prepared in manuscript.

Hour, Date, Place			Summary of Events and Information	Remarks and references to Appendices MAP
3/4m, 14h/w	15-5-16	Grand Ravissage Farm	Drainage of existing Trenches – Deepening same & fixing Iron Frames. Weather – Dark night with continuous rain	B+7 36 C 8 d 4.8 & 2.8 S/R
2nd	15-5-16	La Tuna Tilleule	Filling in for Platform siding – Removing earth & laying out wire. Weather fine	B+7 36 B 2 c 3.6 S/R
1st 4th & 3rd	16-5-16	Grand Ravissage Farm	Drainage of existing Trenches – Wiring Trestle Frames – Fixing Notching. Weather fine	B+7 36 C 8 d 4.8 & 2.7.8 S/R
2nd	16-5-16	La Tuna Tilleule	Filling in for Platform siding – Construction of Dug Roof – Weather fine	B+7 36 B 2 c 3.6 S/R
1st 4th & 3rd	17-5-16	Grand Ravissage Farm	Construction of Brush Thorn Frame – Iron Frames – Wiring Brush – Resetting wire wiring. Weather fine	B+7 36 C 8 d 4.8 & 2.7.8 S/R
2nd	17-5-16	Vicinity of La Touquet Stn	Revetting with corrugated iron a high bank – Sand bag barn – Weather fine.	B+7 36 C 9 b 2 S/R
3rd	17-5-16	La Tuna Tilleule	Road Excavation – Removing earth to make up railway siding – Laying Cupid. Weather fine.	B+7 36 B 2 c 3.6 S/R
1st 4th & 3rd	18-5-16	Vicinity of La Touquet Stn.	Constructing Parados – Strengthening existing Parapet – Driving Stakes – Wiring Parados for attack – Crenalls. I.O.R. bullet wound Knee – Weather misty	B+7 36 C 9 b 2 S/R
1st 4th & 3rd	18-5-16	Grand Ravissage Farm	Sand bag wetting – Drainage & Excavating Trenches – Distant fire attack – Weather very misty.	B+7 36 C 8 c 4.8 d 4.7.8 S/R
2nd	18-5-16	Vicinity La Touquet Stn	Revetting with corrugated iron a large barn – Sand bag revetment Siding bags – Preparing Parapet. Weather fine	B+7 36 C 9 c 2 S/R
3rd	18-5-16	La Tuna Tilleule	Ramming Subsoil – Ramming tar lights railway – Levelling bank on Parados way – Preparing Surface & laying lengths of lights railway. Weather fine	B+7 36 B 2 c 6.3 S/R

(73989) W414/--463. 400,000. 9/14. H.&J.Ltd. Forms/C. 2118/10.

Army Form C. 2118.

WAR DIARY
or
INTELLIGENCE SUMMARY.
(Erase heading not required.)

Instructions regarding War Diaries and Intelligence Summaries are contained in F.S. Regs., Part II and the Staff Manual respectively. Title pages will be prepared in manuscript.

Hour, Date, Place	Summary of Events and Information	Remarks and references to Appendices
10.15h to 18.30hr 19-5-16 Vicinity of Le Touquet Stn	Carrying munition materials — Driving Pickets — Sand bag revetment — wiring up Parapets — Weather fine — Sniping & machine gun fire at intervals.	B+7 36 c g 2 d B/16
14hr to 18hr 19-5-16 Front Redoubt Farm	Sand bag revetment — Excavating — Filling bags. Weather fine	B+7 36 C 8 2 j 8 B/16
6hr to 14hr 19-5-16 Vicinity Le Touquet Str	Sand bag revetment — Completing revetment — Wiring trucks — Weather fine half hour late owing to hostile aeroplane	B+7 36 C g 2 d B/16
15hr to K15hr 19-5-16 La Truie Tilleul	Running subsoil — Ramming — Ditching — Refixing & laying light railway Weather fine	B+7 36 B 22 c 36 B/16
14hr to 18hr 20-5-16 Vicinity of Le Touquet Str	Carrying materials — Strengthening Parapets — Driving Pickets — Weather fine also much machine action	B+7 36 c g 2 d B/16
14hr to K16hr 20-5-16 Front Redoubt Farm	Digging trenches — Sand bag revetment — Wiring — Weather fine	B+7 36 C 8 2j 8 B/16
9hr to K16hr 20-5-16 Le Bizet	Constructing dugouts & Splinter Proof Shelters Weather fine	B+7 36 NW c.13 B/16
8hr to K14hr 20-5-16 Vicinity of Le Touquet Str	Carrying in revetment — Sand bag revetment — wiring back — Weather fine — Work stopped for 20 minutes owing to shell fire. 15 shells returned.	B+7 36 c g 2 d B/16
6.45 to 15hr 20-5-16 La Truie Tilleul	Ramming subsoil — Excavating — Ditching to breaking weight — filling in a running Water pipe	B+7 36 B 22 c 36 B/16
14hr to K12hr 21-5-16 Vicinity of Le Touquet Str	Driving Pickets — Making up & wiring Parapets — area heavily — Weather fine — Catapulted N3 sphere with 30 ox explosive about 100x from Redoubt — no damage	B+7 36 c g 2 d B/16
3.30hr 20-5-16 La Truie Tilleul		B+7 36 B 22 c 36 B/16

(73989) W4141-463. 400,000. 9/14. H.&J.Ltd. Forms/C. 2118/10.

Army Form C. 2118.

WAR DIARY
or
INTELLIGENCE SUMMARY.
(Erase heading not required.)

Instructions regarding War Diaries and Intelligence Summaries are contained in F.S. Regs., Part II. and the Staff Manual respectively. Title pages will be prepared in manuscript.

Hour, Date, Place	Summary of Events and Information	Remarks and references to Appendices
9th hr 20 5th 21-5-16 Pont Rotique	Constructing & erecting framing — throwing up parapets & paradoes — excavating — Weather fine, very warm.	B47 36 C8,9,4,8 MAP 8/6
10 hr 21-5-16 Le Touv Tilloh	Aerial Recce from aeroplane between buildings ? farm — time dropped not known.	B47 36 B22 C36 8/6
8th hr K15 Khd 22-5-16 Le Paris Tilloh	Carrying centonment frames from R.E. Yard — setting out & cutting concrete field work partition — damming top & laying down pipes — shutte-ing in/side — showing in after noon. Weather	B47 36 B22 C36 8/6
9 hr 70/Khd 22-5-16 Le Bizet	Preparing shutters & splintered earth in several different parts of village — Partin of light to take wire frm an aircraft on several positions. Delay by rather showery	B47 36 C13 8/6
8th hr 22 hr 22-5-16 Vicinity Le Touquet Sta	Corrugated iron revetment — Sand bag revetment — Wiring track — Frying frames — filling & carrying sand bags — Weather fine	B47 36 C a 9 82 8/6
21 hr 22 to 2 hr 23-5-16 Vicinity Le Touquet Sta	Building up parapets — Driving Pickets — Weather: bright moonlight — enemy flares numerous & hindersome to men working on Parapets	B47 36 C a 9 82 8/6
20 hr 22 to 2 hr 23-5-16 Pont Rotique	Carrying & fixing Brick Grates in positions — Weather: very bright night	B47 36 C a 8,9, 2,8 8/6
9 hr 10 hr 18 Khd 23-5-16 Le Bizet	Preparing shutters & splinter proofs in village — Weather fine —	B47 36 C13 8/6
8th hr 15 Khd 23-5-16 Vicinity of Le Touquet Sta	Corrugated iron revetment — filling & carrying revetment mat. & sand bags — Wiring track — fixing up shutto — Weather fine	B47 36 C a 9 82 8/6
8th hr 10 hr 22-5-16 Le Tour Tillods	Excavating earth, depositing & ramming for pentroy — Rerring M. forms — Loring light railway to keep dumps.	B47 36 B22 C36 8/6
8th hr 18 hr 23-5-16 Ammunition	3 enemy aeroplanes sighted ordered up during the day, in which Batteries included attempted once & other opened situated near the firing, but british batteries some of them from positions, as heavy shell fire was almost immediately directed on them from OVER	B47 36 C 2 8 3 8/6

WAR DIARY
or
INTELLIGENCE SUMMARY.
(Erase heading not required.)

Army Form C. 2118.

Hour, Date, Place	Summary of Events and Information	Remarks and references to Appendices
18 hrs 23-5-16 Ammunitions (continued)	Reaction of howitzers, he shells passing over their billets & fragments falling in near the quarters. One casualty occurred. They drifted in the gas during attack on Pretrinase & sustaining a sword scalp wound. Still shelling intermittent until about 23 hrs.	B+7 36 C 2.6 a 8.3
5 hrs 24-5-16 Ammunitions	Anti air craft fire again opened fire on Turco enemy bains, which retired. One drove 9 he km the shell fire recommenced, we shell trusting in squares of trenches, incurring 5 O.R. Casualties wound, also two horses wounded.	B+7 36 C 2.6 a 8.3
22 hrs 23rd to 1½ hr 24-5-16 Vicinity of Le Touquet Stn	Carrying material, about 21 cart, now great to trench — During Pickets for wiring — making up &c-work & Cracking Sand Bag revetment. Weather fine, night dark — Many flares & desultory rifle fire.	B+7 36 C A F-R
18 hrs 24-5-16 Ammunitions	Firing to unnecessary rifle incurred by unarming Pickets in front of new received from a vacant Hill Qrs to move to nippe C & D Coy H.Q. on 248 through wood evacuating march in half platoons commencing at 18 hrs 2 in wounded in (C Coy) were able to occupy quarters under cover when not at work.	B+7 36 B 1.6 c 6.9
19 hrs 23rd to 2 hr 24-5-16 Great Rideye farm	Filling Sand bags — securing — day shell fine, 8 wires distributed along length of track. Weather wind & dark.	B+7 36 C 7.4.8 & 1.8
9½ hrs 24-5-16 Vicinity Le Touquet Stn	Sniping continues — Canopies in wire cut — Wing task — filling & carrying sand bags — catting & fixing Stars. Clearing walk way under ankle hard. Weather showery	B+7 36 C 9.6.3
9½ hrs K 1·35 hrs 24-5-16 Le Tour Titlake	Battery has been at road at 45° & turning up an wire 120 yds along hilling to depth 4′ 9″ — Pit bordering roles of site — commenced tapping unused wire casualty 1 O.R. slight — Weather showery from outside Beat	B+7 36 B 2.2 c 2.3
9½ hrs K 1·5 hrs 24-5-16 Le Bizet	Enemy in more or less in stations perfa — Some wiring & snaring B +7 31 air craft active. Weather showery.	B+7 36 C 1.3
10 hrs K 16 hrs 25-5-16 Le Bizet	Work on Army shift & shell point continues — Rifle works & fine.	B+7 36 C 1.3

WAR DIARY
or
INTELLIGENCE SUMMARY.
(Erase heading not required.)

Army Form C. 2118.

Instructions regarding War Diaries and Intelligence Summaries are contained in F.S. Regs., Part II and the Staff Manual respectively. Title pages will be prepared in manuscript.

Hour, Date, Place	Summary of Events and Information	Remarks and references to Appendices MAP
2nd Army 14th Bde 25-5-16 Vicinity of La Touquet Sec.	Digging Pickets — Strengthening Parapets on Park Row — Carrying materials — Weather wet & dark	B7 + 36 C9 & 2 Rifles
14th Bde W.K. 1st Rely 25-5-16 Pont à Rabique Farm	Digging Down P.C. — Filling & Carrying sand bags — Weather wet & night dark	B7 + 36 C6 & 6 21.2 Rifles
1 R.I.R. W.K.13th Rely 25-5-16 Vicinity of La Touquet Sec & firing trenches	Firing, Carrying & Watering with Sand Bags — Wiring back — Weather fine	B7 + 36 C9 & 2 Rifles
Regt W.K. 15th Rely 25-5-16 La Tracé Wk	8 x Country Borrow pits — Carrying earth to make up light Railway — making Dutch — Carrying & laying sleepers for ruct — Taking up & relaying light Railway Setts — Laying railway — Unloading timber trucks — Weather fine	TST 7 36 B22 C63 Rifles
Regt WK 21 Aug 56 Thu 26-5-16 Vicinity of La Touquet Sec	Carrying materials — Burying Pickets — Strengthening Parapets of Parados — Weather very wet & dark, delaying work.	B7 + 36 C9 & 2 Rifles
9th Bde W.K. 16th Relief 26-5-16 Vicinity of La Touquet Sec	Filling, Carrying & waiting with sandbags — Congested in movements — Shivering & wiring back. Weather fine.	BQ + 36 C9 & 2 Rifles
8th Bde W.K. 15th Rely 25-5-16 La Tracé trenches	Trenching — Taking up & relaying Pairs of paving — Loading & carrying clay & laying same in bed to park. Weather fine.	B7 + 36 B22 C6 3 Rifles
14 Rly 21 Bde W.K. 27-5-16 Pont à Rabique Farm	Bearing up light & trench — Sand bag revetment — Work cleared up & material covered up — Weather fine — Dark night	B7 + 36 C6 & 8 21.8 Rifles
2 R.I.R. WK 1 Rely 27-5-16 Vicinity of La Touquet Sec	Carrying Material — Driving Pickets — Making up Parapet — Weather fine — Dark night	B7 + 36 C9 & 2 Rifles
9th Aub W.L. 16th Rely 27-5-16 Vicinity of La Touquet Sec	Congested in movements — Sand bag revetment — Shifting — Wiring back of front Sec dug on 7 Touquet & Le Touquet Sec — Weather fine	BQ + 36 C9 & 2 Rifles
8th Bde WK 15 Rely 27-5-16 La Tracé trenches	Carting Setts — Carting Sleepers — Erecting Trestle Platform & Stacking Timber — Laying Paine & Graveling with Timber — Weather fine	B7 + 36 B22 C63 Rifles

WAR DIARY
or
INTELLIGENCE SUMMARY.
(Erase heading not required.)

Army Form C. 2118.

Hour, Date, Place		Summary of Events and Information	Remarks and references to Appendices
2 hrs 2½ K 16 h2	26-5-16 Warnimont to Torquetot	Carrying materials — Driving Pickets — Thickening Parapet — Trench line — Sniping as usual.	B♣ ↑ 36 C 9 6.2 P16
	27-5-16 Ditto	Trench Garrison A & B Coys, Transport & Band, moved into new billets at Warnimont Farm.	B♣ ↑ 36 B 11 2 6.8 P16
7 hrs K 16 h2	28-5-16 29-5-16 Warnimont to Torquetot	Carrying & Ampro Man materials — Filling Camp & Making Sand Bag revetment — Wiring trench & Shutting. Weather fine. Aeroplane active on both sides.	B♣ ↑ 36 C 9 6.2 P16
7 hrs K 16 h2	29-5-16 Auchin Avenue	Drew Painter employed in town on revetting. Weather fine by day, heavy rain at night.	B♣ ↑ 28 W 14 B 3 P16
21 hrs 29 April 30 5-16	30-5-16 Warnimont to Torquetot	Carrying materials — Thickening Parapet — Cr Checking Trench — Weather wet.	B♣ ↑ 2 9 C 9 6.27 P16
7 hrs K 16 K 16	30-5-16 Ploegstreet Wood	Trench in Shock Farm Withdrawal & deepened from stores West 5 point in trench — Aerial work through 2 & 3 B. Weather had ont. (artillery fire on both sides).	B♣ ↑ 28 M U 26 & 27 P16
7 hrs K 18 hrs 30-5-16 April K 13 hrs 30-5-16 2 hrs 3 hrs 31-5-16	Outain Avenue Warnimont Garrison	Filling in polical trenches - 100 a walling villatrant - improving drainage - Fishing tram from Public employed in town.	B♣ ↑ 26 5th W 14 B P16
8 hrs 16 hrs 31-5-16	Ploegstreet	Sand bag revetment — Excavating 3 dugouts — Consolidated iron revetment — creating draw side walk. Weather fine. 4 H.E. shells falling in wood.	B♣ ↑ 28 5th U 27 6.3.9 P16
13 hrs	31-5-16 Torquetot North	Casualties - 1 man employed in T.trainings killed by shell — 8 Sunther, D coy - shot in the front trench on survey in the trenches.	B♣ ↑ 28 5th U 26 a.5.1 P16
7 hrs K 15 K 16	31-5-16 Ploegstreet Wood	Transfer from Brick Farm to Hunters Avenue entrust of Ploegstreet now Weather fine. Work Mostly interferd with by heavy Shellfire on Stand Corners Camp Prom.	B♣ ↑ 28 5th U 26 & 27 P16

From- Officer Commanding
      19th (S) B'n Middlesex Regt (Pioneers),
      B.E.F.

To-   D.A.G.,
      3rd Echelon, Base.

War Diary for June, 1916.

             Herewith, original copy of
War Diary for June, 1916.

                        A. Hons.
                     Lt Colonel,
                 Commanding 19th (S) B'n
                 Middlesex Regt (Pioneers).

June 30th, 1916.

Army Form C. 2118.

WAR DIARY
or
INTELLIGENCE SUMMARY.
(Erase heading not required.)

Instructions regarding War Diaries and Intelligence Summaries are contained in F. S. Regs., Part II. and the Staff Manual respectively. Title pages will be prepared in manuscript.

(7)

Hour, Date, Place	Summary of Events and Information	Remarks and references to Appendices
Ontario Attack 31-5-16	Excavating Boshen Pits — Sank bog working — Weather fine — Work must Illayed by shellfire	MAP B97 28 SW V14 £ 77 £ 22 8/6 Attacno Lt Colonel Commanding 14th (S) Bn N^dAllenkurpes

19 Middlesex Vol 2

XII
June 1916

WAR DIARY
or
INTELLIGENCE SUMMARY.
(Erase heading not required.)

Army Form C. 2118.

Instructions regarding War Diaries and Intelligence Summaries are contained in F.S. Regs., Part II and the Staff Manual respectively. Title pages will be prepared in manuscript.

Hour, Date, Place	Summary of Events and Information	Remarks and references to Appendices
7hrs 31½hrs 1-6-16 ONTARIO AV. WINNIPEG AV.	Driving – Placing Frame – Excavating Borrow Pits – Filling Sand Bags – Weather fine	Bt 7 26 SW V 14 d 7·7 & 2 8½6
9hrs 15½hrs 1-6-16 PLOEGSTEERT WOOD	Work continued – Trenches widened & deepened to HUNTERS AVENUE – Weather fine – Casualties – Shell shock	Bt 7 28 SW U 26 d 2·7 8½6
6hrs 14hrs 1-6-16 PLOEGSTEERT WOOD	Excavated 185 yds. 3 ft × 2 ft 6 – Cement 10·0 Sqd yds – Weather fine	Bt 7 29 SW U 21 d 3·9 8½6
23½hrs 18½hrs 2-6-16 ONTARIO AV. WINNIPEG AV.	Excavating Borrow Pits – Revetting – Making Bomb Store – Wiring – Camouflet – von wetland – & making frames. Weather fine	Bt 7 26 SW V 14 d 7·7 & 8·2 V 19 d 2·7 8½6
9hrs 16 15½hrs 2-6-16 PLOEGSTEERT WOOD	Work continued – Trenches bottomed & trimmed – Bridging commenced at HUNTERS AV. – Trench side at NORTH HUNTERS AV. – Weather fine – Intermittent shelling throughout day	Bt 7 28 SW U 26 d 2·7 9½6
20hrs 14 hrs 14½hrs 2-6-16 WARNAVE AVENUE	Trenches dug – 90 yds – Weather fine – 60 mm artillery fire but with R.E. on small Matlin implements	Bt 7 28 SW U 17 d 2 8½6
9hrs 16 14hrs 2-6-16 PLOEGSTEERT WOOD	Excavating Trench 1·50 × 2' × 2'9" – Weather fine	Bt 7 28 SW U 21 d 2·9 8½6
18hrs 3-6-16 ONTARIO AV. WINNIPEG AV.	ONT. AV. Excavating Borrow Pits – Revetting – WINN. AV. Making Frames – Placing Panels on Bomb Store – Carrying Parties – Weather fine	Bt 7 26 SW V 14 d 7·7 & 8·2 V 19 d 2·7 8½6
8½hrs K 14 X½ 3-6-16 PLOEGSTEERT WOOD	Bridging in HUNTERS AV. – Trenching at N. HUNTERS AV. – Weather fine – Some shelling during day	Bt 7 28 SW U 26·27 8½6
13½hrs 3-6-16 WARNAVE	107 yards of Trench dug & levelled – Weather fine – Several attempts to overcraft	Bt 7 28 SW U 26 d 7·3 8½6

WAR DIARY or INTELLIGENCE SUMMARY

Army Form C. 2118.

June 1916

Hour, Date	Place	Summary of Events and Information	Remarks and references to Appendices. MAP
8 to 1 pm 3-6-16 D	PLOEGSTEERT WOOD	Excavating Trench 120 ft. 3'×3' — Revetments Trench 300 yds — Wiring materials — Carrying Weather fine	B1.7.728.SW U.21.a.3.9 916
2.0 to 4.30 & 11.30 to 4 am 4-6-16 C	WARNAVE A/	90 yds Trench revetted. Opening mats into CHESHIRE AVENUE. Weather fine, Heavy bombardment in late evening at 0.25 hr.	B4.728.SW U.27.d 916
5.30 to 9 pm 5-6-16 A	ONTARIO AVENUE	Wiring & fixing frames — Revetting with corrugated iron & sand bags — Repairing Trenches — building & unloading materials. Weather showery	B1.7.728.SW U.14.d.7.7 916
8 am to 1 pm 5-6-16 B	PLOEGSTEERT WOOD	Trenching & Revetting to HUNTERS AVENUE — Framing removed. Weather showery	B4.728.SW U.26.b.17 916
7 to 11 am 5-6-16 C	WARNAVE AVENUE	New trench cut, revetted & deepened. Weather Showery	B4.728.SW U.26.a.43 916
8 am to 1 pm 5-6-16 D	PLOEGSTEERT WOOD	Fixing frames — Corrugated iron revetment — 100 sq yds cleared & re-laid — filling sand bags — Excavating. Weather Showery	B4.728.SW U.19.a.3.9 916
2.0 am 6-6-16 C	WARNAVE AVENUE	100 yds of trench deepened & trimmed. Weather wet, dark night, M & fire taste	B4.728.SW U.27.d 916
5 to 10 pm 6-6-16 A	ONTARIO AVENUE	Cutting new Drains — wiring & fixing frames — Revetting iron & sand bags. Work proceeding on Bomb store, placing bricks & sand bags — Weather wet	B1.728.SW U.14.d.7.7 916
7 to 11 am 6-6-16 C	WARNAVE AVENUE	85 yds new Trench cut, deepened & revetted. Weather wet	B4.728.SW U.26.a.7.4 916
7 pm to 1.30 am 6-6-16 D	PLOEGSTEERT WOOD	Clearing undergrowth — Excavating — fixing frames — Filling sand bags — Corrugated iron revetment — commencement of work delayed by weather	B4.728.SW U.21.c.3.9 916

WAR DIARY or INTELLIGENCE SUMMARY.

Army Form C. 2118.

(3) June 1916

(Erase heading not required.)

Hour, Date, Place			Summary of Events and Information	Remarks and references to Appendices
20th 6/6/16 7pm	7-6-16	WARNAVE AVENUE	65 yards of Trench dug — Revetting material carried from Dump — Weather showery — many improvements made in sights between 2.35 & 2.4 hrs — M gun action	B.77.28.SW U.27.2 Ble
5th bn right 7pm	7-6-16	ONTARIO AVENUE	Wining & sixing frames — Chipping bornr hits — increasing earthwork at ONTARIO AVENUE — Loading dump at Bomb store. Weather dull	B.77.28.SW J.14.2.7.7 J.19.2.7.7 Ble
8 Lan L 11 Rift	7-6-16	PLOEGSTEERT WOOD	Trench widened at N. HUNTERS AV. — Fixing frames S. HUNTERS AV. Work continued at ESSEX FARM — Weather dull — considerable shelling in morning. one O.R. casualty. shell shock	B.77.26.SW V.26.27 Ble
15th bn 6/11 Lon	7-6-16	WARNAVE AVENUE	75 yards Trench cut. Revetment & turfline in A.E. Dump & LAWRENCE FARM	B.77.28.SW V.26.2.4.3 Ble
9 bach 11 pm	7-6-16	PLOEGSTEERT WOOD	Carrying knife frames & works sand bags — Ditching & collecting sand bags — Excavating bombing post — Working up levelwork — Weather Dull — Casualties 2 O.R. wounded	B.77.28.SW V.21.63.9 Ble
20th Jul 6/11 Lon	8-6-16	WARNAVE AVENUE	Trench Revetment & widened — Revetting materials brought from Dump & bivelwork along trench — Weather showery — M gun action.	B.77.28.SW U.27.2 Ble
5th bn right 9pm	8-6-16	ONTARIO AVENUE	Excavating bornr pits — fixing frames — fixing duck boards — Weather fine	B.77.28.SW J.14.27.7 Ble
8 Lan L 11 Lan B	8-6-16	PLOEGSTEERT WOOD	Ground work continued N. HUNTERS AV.E & at ESSEX FARM. 25 frames fixed — Work stopped by infantry & artillery action — Weather fine.	B.77.28.SW V.26.47 Ble
15th bn 14th bn 6-6-16	6-6-16	WARNAVE AVENUE	Revetting 150 yds of Trench — Cutting Drain 2.5 yds — Weather fine.	B.77.28.SW V.26.2.4.3 Ble

WAR DIARY
or
INTELLIGENCE SUMMARY.
(Erase heading not required.)

Army Form C. 2118.

June 1916

Hour, Date, Place		Summary of Events and Information	Remarks and references to Appendices
8hrs to 14hrs D	8-6-16 PLOEGSTEERT WOOD	Fixing frames – Corrugated iron revetment – Sand bag revetment – fixing plates – channelling – cleaning ditch – Excavating – fixing dug out frames	B7 F 28 SW V 21 C 3.9 R.E
night	8-6-16	Owing to Artillery operations no night work was done	R.E.
5hrs to 19hrs A	9-6-16 ONTARIO AVENUE	Wiring & fixing frames – corrugated iron revetment – excavating new trench revetment – Weather dull	B7 F 28 SW V 14 a 7.7 R.E
8hrs to 14hrs B	9-6-16 PLOEGSTEERT WOOD	25 frames fixed – Sand work continued by ESSEX FARM & N. HUNTERS AVENUE – Weather dull	B2 F 28 SW V b. 17 R.E
7 khrs to 14hrs C	9-6-16 WARNAVE AVENUE	180 yds trench & ditch – widening trench – Revetting – carrying materials – Weather dull	B9 F 28 SW 26 a 4.3 R.E
8hrs to 14hrs D	9-6-16 PLOEGSTEERT WOOD	2.0 Trench Frames fixed – 7.5" ditch excavated – Pit props & sand bag revetment – filling & carrying sand bags – Weather dull	B7 F 28 SW V 21. C 3.9 R.E
Night	9-6-16	Owing to Artillery operations no night work was done	R.E
5hrs to 19hrs A	10-6-16 ONTARIO & ANSCROFT AVENUES	Wiring & fixing frames – Excavating Comm pits – Putting new frames at ANSCROFT AV. – Weather fine	B7 F 28 SW V 14 a 4.6 R.E
8hrs to 14hrs B	10-6-16 PLOEGSTEERT WOOD	Frames fixed in work – Gun work by ESSEX FARM completed – KEEPERL HUT continued – Some delay owing to fire from our guns – also available shelling – Weather fine	B7 F 28 SW V 26. 27 R.E
7khrs to 20hrs C	10-6-16 WARNAVE AVENUE	45 yds revetment – 280 yds deepened trench – A frame placed in position – Weather fine	B7 F 28 SW V 26 -20 a. 3 R.E
8hrs to 14hrs D	10-6-16 PLOEGSTEERT WOOD	5 dug out frames fixed – corrugated iron & expanded iron revetment – wiring – Excavating – Weather fine	B7 F 28 SW V 21 C 3.9 R.E

June 1916 (5) Army Form C. 2118.

WAR DIARY
or
INTELLIGENCE SUMMARY.
(Erase heading not required.)

Instructions regarding War Diaries and Intelligence Summaries are contained in F.S. Regs., Part II. and the Staff Manual respectively. Title pages will be prepared in manuscript.

Hour, Date, Place		Summary of Events and Information	Remarks and references to Appendices
2nd June to 10th	SUPPORT LINE	60 men & 1 O. Coy attached to R.E. for work on Trench Mortar emplacements daily from 2nd June	A577 26SW U 18 a R/6
9h hr & 19th 11-6-16	WARNAVE AVENUE	Revetting – Trench dugouts & tramway – making & laying Duck Boards LANCASHIRE COTTAGE SHELTER during morning – Weather fine	B 9.47 28 SW U 26 a 4.3 R/6
10 hrs K 11th hr 11-6-16	PLOEGSTEERT WOOD	Filling, carrying & laying Sand Bags – Corrugated iron revetment – Dugouts – Excavating – work C. iron. W rather fine	B3x 9 28 SW U 21 c 3.9 R/6
5th hr & 14 hrs 12-6-16	ONTARIO AVENUE ANSCROFT AVENUE	Cutting out new trench – Completing revetment – Excavating. Wiring & Fixing Frames. W rather wet	A577 28SW U 14 2.4.6 R/6
8 hrs K 14½ hrs 12-6-16	PLOEGSTEERT WOOD	25 Frames fixed – 400 yds Trench S. ESSEX FARM dug 6" deep. Weather wet – Shelling in morning, one O.R. Casualty slight	B 9.47 28 SW U 26.27 R/6
9½ hr & 19½ hr 12-6-16	WARNAVE AVENUE	85 yds Trench deepened & widened – 60 yds Trench revetted. Weather fine	B9.47 28 SW U 26 a 4.3 R/6
9½ hr K 1½ hr 12-6-16	PLOEGSTEERT WOOD	62 Chute corrugated iron fixed – 1 Dug out framed – 600 Sand bags filled – Wiring – Putteting – draining – excavating – Weather Good	B 9.47 28 SW U 21 c 3.9 R/6
5½ hr & 19 hrs 13-6-16	ONTARIO A/ ANSCROFT A	Wiring & fixing Frames, cutting new trench – cutting out trench. Weather dry wet inclining wet	B9.7 25 SW U 14 2.4.6 R/6
9 hrs K 14 hr 15-6-16	PLOEGSTEERT WOOD	Sitting Trench 300 yds – fixing frames – fixing Duck Boards – work delayed by wet weather	B9.47 28 SW U 26.27 R/6
9 hrs K 15½ hr 13-6-16	BORDER RD	Trench Drains, Dugouts & cupolas – Drain cuts – Weather very bad – rain all day	B577 28 SW U 27 c 3.9 R/6

WAR DIARY
or
INTELLIGENCE SUMMARY.
(Erase heading not required.)

Army Form C. 2118.

June 1916

Hour, Date, Place			Summary of Events and Information	Remarks and references to Appendices
8 hrs to 4 pm	13-6-16	PLOEGSTEERT WOOD	Filling & carrying sand bags — During day Pits — Wiring — Corrugated iron — Firing frames — excavating — Weather very wet	B9728SW U21 c 3.9 8/6
7 hrs to 6	14-6-16	ONTARIO & ANSCROFT AV	Wiring & fixing frames — Completing Earthworks & drains — Ripping up French — Weather very wet — Relaying walk — considerable shellfire on ANSCROFT AV. & N.E. thereof — ONTARIO AV. Seen in	B9728SW V14 2 4.6 8/6
6 hrs to 20 hrs	15-6-16	ONTARIO & ANSCROFT AV	Wiring & fixing frames — getting out new work at N end of ONT. AV. — Repairing wire down in by H.E. shell — A NICE AV. Wind → ing frame — Revetting — Weather fair	B9728SW V14 2 4.6 8/6
8 hrs to 13	15-6-16	LOWNDES AV.	Firing frames — Drainage work continued HQ HUNTERS AV. — Found work continued with N & S setting line — Weather fair — Crash work taken on Revetting — (Parked Retaliation)	B9428SW V26 27 8/6
7 hrs to 10/pm	15-6-16	BORDER AVENUE	Trench sides trimmed — Revetting — Firing Duck boards — Wet & tatting — Work impeded by shell fire, also by water & experience of clay	B9728SW V27 c 3.9
8 hrs to 1 b hrs	15-6-16	PLOEGSTEERT WOOD	Excavating — Expanded metal retitting — Corrugated iron, & C.I. R.S.J. watching — Sawing pickets — Weather fine	B9728SW V21 c 3.9 8/6
8 hrs to 20 hrs	16-6-16	ONTARIO & ANSCROFT AV	Wiring & fixing frames — Revetting — Ripping French — Thinning up earth — Canadian AV., 2 ditches and dykes — 3 OR	AMt 26 SW V14 d 4.6 8/6
8 hrs to 14 hrs	16-6-16	PLOEGSTEERT WOOD	4.5 French frames H&C — so ydr Duck boarding fixed — French sides & drains & frequent shelling — near ESSEX FARM — Weather fine —	B9728SW V16 27 8/6
7 hrs to 11 hrs	16-6-16	BORDER AV.	Trench cleaned & trimmed — 50 yds revetted — Weather fine — French shelled — Work stopped early amount of ammunition below	B9728SW V27 c 3.9 8/6
6 hrs to 9	16-6-16	PLOEGSTEERT WOOD	Busying main drain — Sand bag revetment — Exp. metal & corr. iron work — Sawing — Wiring — Laying Duck boards — Weather fine —	B9728SW V21 c 2-9 8/6

WAR DIARY or INTELLIGENCE SUMMARY

Army Form C. 2118.

June 1916

Hour, Date, Place	Summary of Events and Information	Remarks and references to Appendices
15.6.17/16 SUPPORT LINE	30 Men per employed with R.E. on Trench mortar emplacements	MAP B9 & 2.85w V.1 & 0
6½ hr to 2 hr 17-6-16 ONTARIO & ANCROFT AV	Wiring & Wiring Frame — Digging out trench & drains — Revetting — Excavating Grenade Pits — Weather fine	B.7 28 SW V.14 Z.4.6
8 to 18 hr 17-6-16 LOWNDES LANE	Frames fixed — Duck boards fixed — Drainage by KEEPERS not continued. Ground work near ESSEX FARM continued. Weather fine. Two shifts worked on after storm from westerly hot litter can be done tomorrow	B.7. 28 S.W. U 26.27
8 to 18 hr 17-6-16 BORDER AV	Cleaning & Levelling track — 100 yds Revetment — Saving Pickets — Wiring — Weather fine — Two stoppages for hostile aircraft	B.7. 28 SW V.27.C.3.9
8 hr 17-6-16 TILLEUL	D company march from TILLEUL Quarters over by 13. E.S.R.	G OOSTHOVE FARM — New billets bag B.7 Z 36 C.2.C.20.
8½ to 18 hr 18-6-16 ONTARIO & ANCROFT AV	Wiring & fixing frames — Digging Trench — Digging drains — Revetting — Weather fine	B.9 + 2.8 SW V.14 Z 4.6
8½ to 13 hr 18-6-16 PLOEGSTEERT WOOD	Carting timber & materials from DOODS FARM & ARMENTIERES — Putting in raiders WAVERLY St. to HUNTERS AV — Carrying frames to trench — Wallen fine — only a small party able to work in trench so had up to 7/6 in in time C	B.7 28 SW V.20 ~ 27
7½ to 19½ hr 18-6-16 BORDER AV	Laying Duckboards — Revetting — Staking & Wiring — Toying rabbit wire — Weather fine	B.9 + 2.8 SW V.27 C 3.9
8 hr 18-6-16 PLOEGSTEERK WOOD	Filling carrying & laying sandbags — laying Duck boards — Exp. metal & corrugation iron — Wiring — Staking — Weather fine	B.7 28 SW V.21 C 39
SUPPORT LINE	1 O.R. Casualty — Party employed on Trench Mortar emplacements	B.7. 28 SW V.28 C

WAR DIARY
or
INTELLIGENCE SUMMARY.
(Erase heading not required.)

Army Form C. 2118.

June 1916

Hour, Date, Place		Summary of Events and Information	Remarks and references to Appendices
6 to 2pm 19-6-16	ONTARIO & ANNSCROFT AV	Wiring — Firing traverses — Revetting — Laying duck boards — Cutting pickets — Digging trench — Weather fine — Heavy shelling for 1 hr during afternoon stand. Whole night work in ANNSCROFT AV	BEF 28 SW U14 C 2 4 6 Pte
2 to 11pm 19-6-16	LOWNDES LANE	Firing traverses — Laying duck boards — Ground work continued from ESSEX FARM to SUPPORT LINE	BEF 28 SW U 21 27 Pte
7 to 19 pm 19-6-16	BORDER AV	Revetting — Laying duck boards — Wiring — Clearing trench of water — Filling rabbit netting — Some delay on account of shelling on LAWRENCE FARM	BEF 28 SW U 27 C 3 - 9 Pte
8 to 11pm 19-6-16	PLOEGSTEERT WOOD	Firing traverses — Corrugated iron & expanded metal revetment — Staking & excavating — Filling & camping sand bags — Weather fine	BEF 28 SW U 21 C 3 - 9 Pte
1 to 5.20 am 20-6-16	ONTARIO & ANNSCROFT AV	Wiring & Firing traverses — Cutting into trench — Draining — Revetting — Excavating — Laying duck boards	BEF 28 SW U 14 A 4 6 Pte
9 to 11pm 20-6-16	LOWNDES LANE	Firing traverses Laying duck boards — Digging trench — Finish work on trench SR of ESSEX FARM — Weather fine. Some shelling early morning.	BEF 28 SW U 26 27 Pte
8 to 10.30pm 20-6-16	BORDER AV	Revetting — Wire & Staking — Tramming trench — Carrying material from Dump — Weather fine. Some shelling	BEF 28 SW U 47 C 7 8 9 Pte
6 to 11 am 21-6-16	PLOEGSTEERT WOOD	Corrugated iron expanded metal & sand bag revetting — Staking — Wiring — Dugout frames & trench frames excavating — Getting trench — Weather fine	BEF 28 SW U 21 C 3 7 9 Pte
6 to 20 pm 22-6-16	ONTARIO & ANNSCROFT AV	Wiring & Windy pipes — Revetting — Deepening borrow pits — Laying duck boards — Weather fine	BEF 28 SW U14 A 4 6 Pte
6 to 11 pm 22-6-16	PLOEGSTEERT WOOD	Firing traverses — Laying duck boards — Ground work continued by supports trench — Considerable shelling / work on ablutes — Weather fine	BEF 28 SW U 26 27 Pte

WAR DIARY or INTELLIGENCE SUMMARY.

Army Form C. 2118.

June 1916.

(Erase heading not required.)

Instructions regarding War Diaries and Intelligence Summaries are contained in F.S. Regs., Part II. and the Staff Manual respectively. Title pages will be prepared in manuscript.

Hour, Date, Place		Summary of Events and Information	Remarks and references to Appendices
1st Pltn	22-6-16	BORDER AV	Entrance cut – Rabbit wiring – Driving Pickets – Wiring back – Revetting – cleaning & burying trench – Weather fine – Tunnel & dugout trenches	B&4 28 SW U 27 C 3.9 Sll
2nd Pltn	22-6-16	PLOEGSTEERT WOOD	Firing Trench & Dug out trenches – Carrying etc. material, Sand Bags – Revetting – Driving & Wiring Pickets – Laying Duck Boards – Clearing – Weather fine	B&4 28 SW U 21 C 3.9 Sll
3rd Pltn	23-6-16	ONTARIO + ANNS(ROFT AV	Wiring of firing trench – Laying Duck boards – Deepening Boram pits – Weather fine	B&4 28 SW U 14 Z m 6 Sll
4th Pltn	23-6-16	PLOEGSTEERT WOOD	Firing trench frames – Laying Duck boards – Wire Entanglement commenced (front) work from HANTS FARM continued – Weather fine	B&4 28 SW V 26 27 Sll
5th Pltn	23-6-16	BORDER AV	Erecting Machine Gun Emplacement – Dugouts cleared – Revetting, mining trench – Weather fine – Shelling at LAWRENCE FM not in trench	B&4 28 SW V 27 C 3.5 Sll
6th Pltn	24-6-16	PLOEGSTEERT WOOD	6 Hunter – Shoring up Parapets work – Firing frames – Carrying in materials – Wiring a Picketing – Walking pm made – filling & laying sandbags	R&4 28 SW U 21 C 3.9 Sll
7th Pltn	20 Lu 24-6-16	ONTARIO + ANNSCROFT A	Wiring of firing frames – Laying sandbags – Laying Duck boards – Work on TRAM M N end of ONTARIO AV – Weather very wet – Heavy shelling Zelugd work – N. end of ONTARIO AV from 11 to 2 pm by H.E.	B+ 28 SW V 14 Z 2.4.6 Sll
8th Pltn	10 Lu 24-6-16	PLOEGSTEERT WOOD	Firing frames – Revett work in DEAD MANS WOOD commenced – Dump trenches in Carried – Faring work by HANTS FARM continued – written wet – 56 shells fell near trench only 1 in any 6 burst: work not recommenced	B+ 28 SW V 26.27 Sll
9th Pltn	19 Lu 24-6-16	BORDER AV	Revetting – Wiring trench – Rabbits wiring – Stoking – Laying Duck boards – work on M.G. Emplacement – Weather very wet	B+ 28 SW D 17 C 3.9 Sll
10th Pltn	24-6-16	PLOEGSTEERT WOOD	Firing Trench frames or corrugation – Driving Pickets & Wiring – laying Sand Bags – 15 ft top drain laid – 95 ft Duck board laid – Weather very wet	B+ 28 SW U 21 C 3.9 Sll

Army Form C. 2118.

June 1916

WAR DIARY or INTELLIGENCE SUMMARY.
(Erase heading not required.)

Instructions regarding War Diaries and Intelligence Summaries are contained in F.S. Regs., Part II and the Staff Manual respectively. Title pages will be prepared in manuscript.

	Hour, Date, Place	Summary of Events and Information	Remarks and references to Appendices
A	18–24hr 6-16 SUPPORT LINE	60 men 5? Cy employed with R.E. on Trench main improvements from 18–24-6-16, + 3.0.g D Coy from 18 to 22-6-16. — 1 O.R. Casualty 18-1-16	B.P.F. 28 S.W V 28 a
B	8.16 to 2hrs 25-6-16 ONTARIO & ANNECRAFT AV	Wiring Cork — Bomb bay wiring — Repairing trench in ONTARIO AV Damaged by H.E. — Deepening trench Pits — Incompleting revetments in ANNECRAFT AV — Work delayed by shelling. Stops to exit in both trenches — Weather fine	B.P.F. 7 28 S.W U14 a 4.6
C	7 k 14hrs 25-6-16 PLOEGSTEERT WOOD	Carting & Carrying materials — It was necessary to allow a day for the men to get fresh supplies of common rifle & grenades in Eng Front.	B.P.F. 28 S.W U 26-27
D	7 k 14hr 25-6-16 BORDER AVENUE	Revetting — Retters Wiring — Filled in Parapet & Erection — Work on M.G. Emplam made — Laying Duck boards — Carrying material up HIGHLAND RD — Weather fine — Work interrupted by shelling fire	B.P.F. 18 S.W U 27 c 39
E	6 14hr 25-6-16 PLOEGSTEERT (WOOD)	Joining Trench pumps — Burying & Wiring Picket — Corn Wire. exp. metal + Shps — Revetment — Excavation — Laying Duck boards & Box drains — Weather fine	B.P.F. 28 S.W V 21 c 3.9
F.G.	103hrs 25-6-16 OOSTHOVE FARM	17 Shells in the Batt H.Q. + their huts — Apparently many registering on Buildings — 1 O.R. Casualty — Unoccupied in huts	B.P.F. 28 S.W 3 11 2 5-7
A	14 to 20hrs 26-6-16 ONTARIO & ANNECRAFT AV	Sand bag revetting — Laying Duck boards — Deepening Bomb Pits — Pickt — Weather unsettled.	B.P.F. 28 S.W U14 2.4.6
B	9 k 14.½ hrs 26-6-16 PLOEGSTEERT (WOOD)	Fixing frames — Drainage & fascine Work continued by SUPPORT LINE — Back-ing unless @8 hr work — Parties under shell fire whilst proceeding to work	B.M.P. 28 S.W V 26 27
C	7 k 10 pm 26-6-16 BORDER AVENUE	Rabbit wire — Being Cont — Pickets — Lay out Duck boards — Carrying material — filling in Parapet — Weather unsettled — Work delayed by rain & shell fire	B.M.P. 28 S.W U 27 c 39
D	8 k 14pm 26-6-16 PLOEGSTEERT (WOOD)	Fixing frames — Pickle driver & wire — Corn wire, exp metal + sand bags — Revetment — Decauville — Laying duck boards — Digging drainage trenches — Weather unsettled — But fine	S.M.P. 28 S.W V 21 c 39

(73989) W4141–463. 400,000. 9/14. H.&J.Ltd. Forms/C. 2118/10.

10

WAR DIARY or INTELLIGENCE SUMMARY.

Army Form C. 2118.

June 1916

Hour, Date, Place	Summary of Events and Information	Remarks and references to Appendices
15 hrs / 26-6-16 / OOSTHOVE FARM HQ	Enemy's artillery registered on huts SW of farm buildings — no direct hits in vicinity — about 10 rounds were fired	B47 3 6 / B11 d 5.7 / 8L
16 to 20 hrs / 27-6-16 / ONTARIO & ANNICROFT AV	Wiring & firing frames — Sandbags & Bother Pits — Wiring — continuous shelling with H.E. & shrapnel necessitated discontinuance of work between the hrs of 16 & 19 in both trenches	B47.2 28W / U 19 2.4.6 / 8L
6 to 14 hrs / 27-6-16 / PLOEGSTEERT WOOD	Fixing Frames — Widening of Trench continued N of HUNTERS FARM — Drainage. General work continued to SUPPORT LINE — Weather wet — some shelling early	B47.2 65W / U 26 2.8 / 8L
7 to 6 / 15 hrs / 27-6-16 / BORDER AV.	Driving & Wiring Pickets — making on the exits to Trench — Weather wet — some delay on account of shell fire	B47.2 65W / U 17 c 3 9 / 8L
6 to 17 hrs / 27-6-16 / PLOEGSTEERT WOOD	Fixing Frames — Cont. work exp. into a sand bag revetment — Driving & Wiring Pickets / 1 Box drawn a 1 Bag at frame trench — excavation — Building Knostern — weather wet	B47.2 65W / B49.2 28W / U 21 c 3 9 / 8L
6 to 20 hrs / 29-6-16 / ONTARIO & ANNICROFT AV	Sand Bag revetment — Repairing French damaged by H.E. — Bother Pits — Weather dull	B47 285W / U 14 2 2.4 / 8L
8 to 14 hrs / 29-6-16 / PLOEGSTEERT WOOD	Fixing Frames — Backlines continued — Work on crossing at HUNTERS AV & ground work on SUPPORT LINE continued — Weather dull	B47.2 28W / U 26 2 7 / 8L
7 to 20 hrs / 29-6-16 / BORDER AVENUE	Rustic Wiring — Covering lawn — Revetting — Picketing & Wiring — 2 entrances cut — LAWRENCE FARM shelled Weather dull	B47 28 5W / V 27 c 3 9 / 8L
6 to 14 hrs / 29-6-16 / PLOEGSTEERT WOOD	Sand Bag complete use of by water revetment — Fixing Frames — excavation — Box drawing Pickets driven & Wired — Weather dull	B47.285W / U 21 c 3 9 / 8L
— / 30-6-16 / OOSTHOVE FARM	Work in Camp owing to I in front schemes	B47 3 6 / B 11 d 5 7 / 8L

A. J. Thomas

Comdg. 1st (S) Bn MAX Regt Kent Cox

I

O.C., 19th (P.W.P.) Bn. Middlesex Regt.

Please cause the first sheet of A.F. 0.2118 to show clearly the name of the unit, and also sign the last sheet (Commanding Officer only).

R E Halcomb
Major,
D.A.A. & Q.M.G.,
41st Division.

M 83.

31/7/1916.

To:- H.Q., 41st Division, A.

II

Amended and returned.

August 1st, 1916.

A. I. Irons
LT. COLONEL.
COMMANDING 19TH (S) BN.
MIDDLESEX REGT. (PIONEERS.)

(8)

Secret.

From: Officer Commanding
19th (S) B'n Middlesex Regt (Pioneers),
B.E.F.

To: Headquarters,
41st Division, G.

War Diary for July, 1916.

Herewith, original copy of War Diary for July, 1916.

A.J. Irons
Lt Colonel,
Commanding 19th (S) B'n
Middlesex Regt (Pioneers).

July 31st, 1916.

4th 2 full
19th (S) Bn. Middlesex Regiment (Pioneers)
July 1916
19. Middlesex

Army Form C. 2118.

WAR DIARY
or
INTELLIGENCE SUMMARY.
(Erase heading not required.)

Instructions regarding War Diaries and Intelligence Summaries are contained in F.S. Regs., Part II and the Staff Manual respectively. Title pages will be prepared in manuscript.

Hour, Date, Place	Summary of Events and Information	Remarks and references to Appendices
6½ to 6.20 A.M. 1-7-16 ONTARIO & ANNSCROFT AV	Corrugated iron & sand bag revetment – Relaying Ramps to trench – Trench for railway – Weather fine	B.7 28 SW U.14 a 7 & 42 B/6
6 to 1 P.M. 1-7-16 LOWNDES AV & HANTS FARM	Firing Frame – Laying Duck boarding – Backing continued – Weather fine	B.7 28 SW U.26 c.4.8 B/6
8 to 12.30 PM 1-7-16 LEWISHAM AV	Digging Trench – Deepening Trench – Weather fine	B.7 28 SW U.15 c.5.5 B/6
8 to 1 PM 1-7-16 PLOEGSTEERT WOOD	Corrugated iron & sand bag revetment – Driving & Wiring Pickets – Excavation – Trig Frame, Duck boards & Box shelter – Weather fine	B.7 28 SW U.21 c.3.9 B/6
10½ AM 1-7-16 GOSTHOVE FARM	Bullet shelters – One direct hit in water tank – 2 o.r casualties slight	B.7 36 B.11 3.5.8 B/6
6½ to 6.20 PM 2-7-16 ONTARIO & ANNSCROFT AV	Corrugated iron & Sand bag revetment – Laying Duck boards – Trenching new trench – Weather fine	B.7 28 SW U.14 a 2.4 B/6
6 to 1 PM 2-7-16 LOWNDES & HUNTERS AV	Firing Frame – Duck boarding – Backing continued – Junction of LOWNDES & HUNTERS AV completed – Weather fine	B.7 28 SW U.26 c.4.8 B/6
8 to 12.30 PM 2-7-16 LEWISHAM AV	Deepening & Widening trench – Weather fine – Work interrupted by thunder-storm & heavy Rain	B.7 28 SW U.15 c.5.5 B/6
8 to 1 PM 2-7-16 PLOEGSTEERT WOOD	Corrugated iron & exp. metal revetment – Laying Duckboards – Driving Wiring Pickets – Box shelter – Filling sandbags – Trail frame – Weather fine	B.7 28 SW U.21 c 3.9 B/6
8 to 11 PM 3-7-16 ONTARIO & ANNSCROFT AV	Firing Frame – Duggery Trenches – Sand bags & 18 man box – Weather fine	B.7 28 SW U.14 a.2.4 B/6
6 to 11 PM 3-7-16 LOWNDES & HUNTERS AV	Firing Frame – Laying Duck boards – Nutting & backing continued – Training at HANTS FARM – Weather fine – Work hindered by heavy showers	B.7 28 SW U.26 c.4.8 B/6
6 to 11 PM 3-7-16 LEWISHAM AV	Trench dug, deepened & widened – Weather fine	B.7 28 SW U.15 c.5.5 B/6
6 to 11 PM 3-7-16 PLOEGSTEERT WOOD	Put up firing frame & wire – Sinking dug outs from excavation – Weather fine	B.7 28 SW U.21 c.3.9 B/6

Army Form C. 2118.

July 1916

WAR DIARY
or
INTELLIGENCE SUMMARY.
(Erase heading not required.)

Instructions regarding War Diaries and Intelligence Summaries are contained in F. S. Regs., Part II. and the Staff Manual respectively. Title pages will be prepared in manuscript.

Hour, Date, Place		Summary of Events and Information	Remarks and references to Appendices
16 to 4pm 4-7-16	ONTARIO & ANASEROFT AV	Wiring — Trench frames — Laying Duck Boards — Excavation — Sand bag revetment — weather wet — work delayed by rain & shell fire	B.M. 2nd SW U14 d 4.6 8/6
8 to 11pm 4-7-16	LOWNDES AV & HUNTERS AV	Filling frames — Laying Duck boards — Retteering & packing entrance — Drainage trenches O.C. entrance at HANTS FARM — Weather very wet	B.M. 2nd SW U26 c 4.8 8/6
8 to 11pm 4-7-16	P.L.O. EASTERN WOOD	Fixing Trench & dugout frames — Carrying Revetment materials up from P.L.O. pump. Fixing — Risgard wire rhylon — excavation — Weather wet	B.M. 2nd SW U21 c 2.9 8/6
6 to 9pm 5-7-16	ONTARIO & ANASEROFT AV	Digging new Trench — wiring & fixing frames — Sand bag revetment — excavation — Some delay from hostile fire — weather fine	B.M. 2nd SW U19 d 2.4 8/6
6 to 11pm 6-7-16	LOWNDES AV	Fixing frames — Laying Duck boards — Putting up & fixing materials — M.G. emplacement commenced by HANTS FARM — Delay caused by enemy aircrafts & by enemy fire at our ack ack	B.M. 2nd SW U26 b c 4.8 8/6
7 to 11.30 5-7-16	THE ONLY WAY	100 yds Trench wire & deepened — weather fine & afternoon	B.M. 2nd SW U15 c 2.5 8/6
8 to 11pm 6-7-16	PUSSEYSTEERT WOOD	Laying Duck boards — Driving & Wiring P/S hoops — Fixing Trench & Dugout frames — excavation — Weather fine wreckage	B.M. 2nd SW U14 c 3.9 8/6
10 to 2am 7-7-16	PRETORIA WAY	50 yds Trench Revetted & deepened in wiring — night firm	T.B. BM 2nd SW U14 C 5.? 8/6
0.15 to 3.0am 7-7-16	ONTARIO & ANACROFT AV	Digging Trench Wiring — Fixing frames — Sand bag revetment — Ration very wet	B.M. 2nd SW U14 d 3.4 8/6
9 to 13pm 7-7-16	LOWNDES AV	Fixing Frames — Laying Duck boards — Setting & packing materials — New Trench between LOWNDES LANE & Support line commenced — Weather wet delaying work	B.M. 2nd SW U26 4.6 8/6
8 to 12.30am 7-7-16	PRETRIM WAY	150 yds Trench deepened & widened — weather wet	B.M. 2nd SW U14 c 5.? 8/6

(73989) W4141—463. 400,000. 9/14. H.&J.Ltd. Forms/C. 2118/10.

WAR DIARY
or
INTELLIGENCE SUMMARY
(Erase heading not required.)

Army Form C. 2118.

July 1916 (3)

Hour, Date, Place	Summary of Events and Information	Remarks and references to Appendices
2:10 hrs 7-7-16 PLOEGSTEERT WD	Digging & Wiring Pit Pipes – Laying Duck boards – Fixing Frames & Dugouts – Fixing Sand bag Curtains to exp. metal sheets – Exploration. Weather showery	B37 28SW V21 C39
2 hrs 8-7-16 TRAMWAY	Trench reference summarised on sketch – Framed different Lengths	B37 28SW V14 C57
16 & 2 hrs 8-7-16 ONTARIO AV N&S	Dragged new trench – Wiring & fixing Frames – Boring Pits – Sand bags – Weather unsettled	B37 28SW V19 D24
8 & 14 hrs 8-7-16 LOWNDES AV	Fixing Frames, Laying Duck boards – Wiring – Setting of Trench matter of Backing Face of CT Support line – Sand bags in trench – CTs left extra wind & damp filling	B37 28SW D26 F48
16 & 13 hrs 8-7-16 THE ONLY WAY	200 yds Trench deepened & widened – Duckboard laid – filling – weather unsettled	B37 28SW V14 C57
8 hrs 8-7-16 PLOEGSTEERT WOOD	Renewing tree roots – cleaning water ditches – Boring & water Pits – fixing Frames – Laying Duck boards	B37 28SW V14 C39
16 & 2 hrs 9-7-16 ONTARIO AV N&S	Draining new trench – Wiring & fixing Frames – Laying Duck boards – filling Bomb Pits & laying same – Weather fine	B37 28SW V19 D24
2 hrs 9-7-16 LOWNDES AV	Carrying materials – Preparing for water of trench trenches by duckhill Pin	B37 28SW D26 F48
16 & 13 hrs 9-7-16 THE ONLY WAY	Cutting 20 yrs open trench – Burrowing – Transportation material – Weather – white interrupted by Enemy Gunfire & Shelling	B37 28SW V14 C52
14 hrs 9-7-16 TORONTO AV	Draining trench & Dugout Floors – Cov Com. wpc metal to sand bag level – Riving & laying Pipes – Drainage on water shown	B37 28SW V21 C39

Army Form C. 2118.

WAR DIARY
or
INTELLIGENCE SUMMARY.
(Erase heading not required.)

July 1916

Hour, Date, Place		Summary of Events and Information	Remarks and references to Appendices
7.6 to 8 hrs	10.7.16 ONTARIO AV N.Y.S	Repairing wire extension by M.E. – Laying Duck board – Sentry over work – Boman pick – Weather fine	BM 2 & SW U19 a 2.4 8/16
7.16 to 16 hrs 10 mins	10.7.16 LOWNDES AV	Putting frames – Laying Duck boards – Burying cable in one of bay in Batteries. Trench continued – filing sand bags	BM 2 & SW U26 b 4.8 8/16
7.16 to 13 hrs	10.7.16 THE ONLY WAY	100 yds Revetment – Trench deepened – work stopped several times to hostile air craft	BM 2 & SW U14 c 5.2 8/16
7.16 to 14 hrs	10.7.16 TORONTO AV	For a tank of Dugout filled – Driving & wiring Pickets – Con iron & dark bays continued – Excavation – Laying duck boards – carrying material	BM 2 & SW U21 c 3.9 8/16
7.16 to 10 hrs	11.7.16 ONTARIO AV N.Y.S	Laying Duck boards – Sand bag revetment – Earth works – excavating – Boman pick – weather fine	BM 2 & SW U14 Z 2.4 8/16
7.16 to 10 hrs	11.7.16 LOWNDES AV	Opening up top of HAMPSHIRE LANE completed – Putting frames – Laying Duck boards – putting & cabling continued – Trench in front of SUPPORTS continued	BM 4 & 18 SW U26 a 2, c 8/16
7.16 to 13 hrs	11.7.16 ONLY WAY	100 yds Revetment – Trench cleared – Detain wrought up – shells Passed us up once – may	BM 18 SW U14 c 5.2 8/16
6.16 to 15 hrs	11.7.16 TORONTO AV	Putting frames – Revetting – Driving & wiring Pickets – 1 Gas dugout – carrying Duck boards – Excavation	BM 2 & SW U21 C 3.9 8/16
6.15 to 15 hrs	13.7.16 ONTARIO AV N.Y.S	Work on Dump Pits & Sand bags – Weather fine – 2nd Party carrying R.E.	BM 2 & SW J19.2.3.10 8/16
4.10 to 5 hrs	13.7.16 LOWNDES AV	Putting frames – Laying Duck boards – Nothing & Bombing continued – Quantity R.F.O. Trench begun 11.50 hrs.	BM 2 & SW J26 a 6, c 2, b 8/16
7.6 to 13 hrs	13.7.16 ONLY WAY	60 yds revetment completed – 35 yds new Duck sub – Weather fine	BM 2 & SW U14 c 5 8/16
7.6 to 14 hrs	13.7.16 TORONTO AV	Putting frames & Dugout frames – Con iron & match & dark bays – Driving & wiring Picket, – Laying Duck B.	BM 2 & SW U21 c 3.9 8/16

WAR DIARY
or
INTELLIGENCE SUMMARY.
(Erase heading not required.)

Army Form C. 2118.

July 1916

Hour, Date, Place	Summary of Events and Information	Remarks and references to Appendices
8.15–12 Thu 14-7-16 / ONTARIO AV N9S	Digging at ISONZO Rd — Sand bag revetment — Repairing Trench — Bombing posts cancelled by R.E. as unsafe at Zipping. H.E. — weather fine — Baths in camp	BM 1658 U16a 2.4 R/6
7.15 p.m Thu 14-7-16 / LOWNDES LANE	Firing parties — Nutting & bathing continued — laying duck boards. KEEPERS HUT BREASTWORK continues — Work stopped at 11.15 on account of rain.	BM 1658 U26a&c0174 R/6
7.45–1.30a.m Thu 14-7-16 / ONLY WAY	Trench work, dugouts & withdrawal — Revetting — Picketing & wiring. Weather fine	BM 1658 U14 c 5.2 R/6
8.6 11 p.m Thu 14-7-16 / TORONTO AV	Firing Trench & Dugout Frames — C. Sav. trip makes & hut requirements. Picketing & wiring — Excavation — Duck boards — Work delayed by shells	BM 1658 U14 c 3.9 R/6
6.5 to 10 p.m 15-7-16 / ONTARIO AV N9S	Sand bag revetment — getting out stones — Bomb pits — Weather fine	BM 1658 U19 2.4 R/6
7.15–6.15 a.m Fri 15-7-16 / LOWNDES LANE	Jib with Horse Duck Boards — Nutting & bathing continues — Three openings mode from Breastworks behind its front — mode in front of KEEPERS HUT withdrawn at 12 hours owing to heavy fire	BM 1658 U26a&c2748 R/6
7.15 12.30 15-7-16 / ONLY WAY	Trenches revetments, wiring & work — Picket drawn — several Islam fires by enemy	BM 2858 V14 c 6.2 R/6
8.6 14 pm 15-7-16 / TORONTO AV	Firing Trench — Wiring & Wiring Pickets — Laying Duck Boards — C. Sav. cks heads — 40 men carrying material	BM 2658 V21 c 3.9 R/6
8.5 to 10 p.m 16-7-16 / ONTARIO AV	Work on Trench Rd & Comm Bags — Work stopped for investigation	BM 1658 U19 2.4 R/6
6 to 20 17-7-16 / ONTARIO AV	Bomb pits — Sand bag revetments — Weather fine	BM 2658 U14 2.16 R/6
7.15 to 12.30 17-7-16 / LOWNDES AV	Firing Horse — Laying Duck Boards — Nutting & bathing continued — was one third withdrawn — Three openings made — Men in front of HUNTER AV withdrawn my whole party, withdrawn at 12th hour for heavy return	BM 2658 U15&c 2754 R/6

(73989) W.4141-463. 400,000. 9/14. H.&J.Ltd. Forms/C. 2118/10.

July 1916 (6)

Army Form C. 2118.

WAR DIARY
or
INTELLIGENCE SUMMARY.
(Erase heading not required.)

Hour, Date, Place		Summary of Events and Information	Remarks and references to Appendices
7.6.12.5hr 17.7.16	ONLY WAY	Revetting – Picketting – Wiring back – laying Duck boards – Carrying material – Heavy Shrapnel during day to work.	B.T.T.2.S.W U.14.c.52 ptt
8hr 16/8hr 17.7.16	TORONTO AV HILL 63	Firing range – C.Coy, experiences 8.5 hrs working – driving & wiring pickets – laying duck boards – carrying material for new trench H.11.60	B.T.T.2.S.W U.15.c.33 ptt
20hr 1st Pk 18.7.16 C	ONLY WAY	Deepening & widening Trench – carrying material – revetting – cleaning Ramsgate trench – M.G. fire along lines at two minute intervals	B.T.T.2.S.W V.14.A.65 ptt
7G 20hr 18.7.16 A	ONTARIO AV	Sand Bag revetment – laying Duck boards – excavating Bollan Tails	B.T.T.2.S.W V.14.d.24 ptt
7G 1.15hr 18.7.16 B	LOWNDES AV	Firing Range – laying Duck boards – carrying material from dump.	B.T.T.2.S.W V.26.A.AC.4.A.6 ptt
7hr 15hr 18.7.16 B	MOULIN DELA RABEQUE FM	2T mnds mortar implements – 2 Shell Stores – Communication Dug between each	B.T.T. 26 C.4.n
7G 13hr 18.7.16	ONLY WAY	Revetting – driving & wiring Pickets – laying duck boards –	B.T.T.2.S.W U.14.c.52 ptt
8G 14hr 18.7.16 D	TORONTO AV HILL 63	Excavation – laying duck boards – carrying materials – new men employed in trench implements	B.T.T.2.S.W U.15.c.33 ptt
2hr 1Pk 19.7.16 E	ONLY WAY	Trench deepened & widened – 25 yds revetments – rifles fire – night work	B.T.T.2.S.W V.14.c.6.2 ptt
6G 20hr 20.7.16 A	ONTARIO AV	Sand bag revetment – excavating Ramsgate Pits – laying Duck boards	B.T.T.2.S.W V.14.d.2.4 ptt
5hr 15.16hr 19.7.16 B	MOULIN DELA RABEQUE FARM	Trench mortar implements & Shell store – revetting & Framing with pair posts & iron grills – sheaving practice worked	B.T.T. 36 C.4.a ptt
7G 16/16hr 19.7.16	MOULIN DELA RABEQUE FARM	Two implements & Shell Store worked by work parties & sand bags – no men employed carrying – work hire delayed by lack of material which came up at night	B.T.T. 26 C.4.a ptt

WAR DIARY
or
INTELLIGENCE SUMMARY.
(Erase heading not required.)

Army Form C. 2118.

July 1916

Hour, Date, Place		Summary of Events and Information	Remarks and references to Appendices
7 to 13hr 20-7-16 C	ONLY WAY	Revetting - Driving & Wiring Pickets - Laying Duck Boards - Weather fine	BTP 28 SW U14 C.5.2 8/16
8 to 4pm 20.7.16 A	TORONTO AV HILL 63	Fixing Frames - Excavation - Laying Duck Boards - Carrying material from Adv E Dump - Work interrupted by shell fire - 20 men working in Trench 81	BTP 28 SW U16 C.9.3 8/16
20 hrs to 4 t/hr 21.7.16 C	ONLY WAY	60 yards Trench duckboard & widened - Weather fine - Shell fire	BTP 28 SW V14 C.5.2 8/16
64 to 20 hrs 21.7.16 A	ONTARIO LOOP ONTARIO AVENUE	Digging new Trench - Wiring & fixing Frames at LOOP - Scantling revetments - Laying Duck boards at AV.	BTP 28 SW V14 2.4 8/16
7 to 18 hrs 22.7.16 D	MOULIN DE LA RABEQUE FARM	Observation post commenced - Carrying frames - Fixing huts on two pits at Station - Delayed by shell fire	BTP 3 6 C 4.2 8/16
7 to 15 hrs 21.7.16 B	ONLY WAY	Revetting - Driving & Wiring Pickets - Laying Duck boards - Weather fine	BTP 28 SW U14 C 5.2 8/16
8 to 14hrs 21.7.16 D	TORONTO AV HILL 63	Excavation - Fixing Frames - Carrying iron revetment - Laying steel tracks - Carrying material - Work interrupted by shell fire	BTP 28 SW U15 C 3.3 8/16
20hrs to 4 t/hr 22.7.16 C	ONLY WAY	25 yds Trench duckboard & widened - 40 yds revetted - Carrying material - Some M.G. fire	BTP 28 SW V14 C.5.2 8/16
14 to 20 hrs 22.7.16 A	ONTARIO AV + LOOP	Wiring & fixing Frames - Digging Trench - Smith Corp revetment - Weather fine	BTP 28 SW V14 2.4 8/16
7.30 to 6 t/hr 23.7.16 B	MOULIN DE LA RABEQUE FARM LOWNDES AV	Two revetments completed - One in progress - Observation Post worked in at RABEQUE FARM 21 Frames fixed at LOWNDES AV -	BTP 36 C 4 & 28 SW V26 & C.274 8/16
7 to 13 hrs 22.7.16 B	ONLY WAY	Driving & Wiring Pickets - Revetting - Laying Duck Boards - 1 hour delay as work was to shell fire.	BTP 28 SW V14 C.5.2 8/16
8 to 16 hrs 22.7.16	TORONTO AV HILL 63	Fixing Frames - Corr iron revetment - Digging Trench - Pumping water from trench - Carrying material - - - travel mortar emplacements	BTP 28 SW V15 C.3.3 8/16

Army Form C. 2118.

WAR DIARY
~~INTELLIGENCE SUMMARY.~~
(Erase heading not required.)

July 1916

Hour, Date, Place	Summary of Events and Information	Remarks and references to Appendices
6 & 2 John 23.7.16 ONTARIO AVP & AV	Wiring & fixing frames – Cross man & sand bag revets – Digging trench – Wicket fire – Zero point	B37+28SW V.14 c.2.14
2 C 15 & 1 thus 23.7.16 11 thus 6.15PM ONLY WAY	Wiring revets – Revetting – Deepening & widening trench – Carrying materials	B37+28SW V.14 c.5.2
8 G 14hrs 23.7.16 TORONTO AV HILL 63	Fixing frames – Fixing car shuts – Laying duck boards – Carrying materials 100 men on trench mortar emplacements	B37+28SW U.15 c.13
24 G John 4.4 7/16 ONTARIO AV & LOOP	Digging out trench – Wiring & fixing frames – Zero point – Earthwork – Sandbags fire cutting flue	13S7+2 & SW V.17 c.2.14
7 C B 14 thus 24.7/16 McDELARADSOUE FARM 4 LOWNDES AV	Observation post completed. Thirst emplacement & bomb store not far – Save bays placed at 25ft & 3rd practice stopped by rain	B4+36 C.4.46 B37+28SW U.26 c.27
7 & 16 13 thus 24.7/16 ONLY WAY	50 yds duck boarding laid – 35 yds revetment – Wiring track	B37+28SW V.17 c.5.2
8G 14hrs 24.7.16 TORONTO AV HILL 63	Fixing frames – Cross war revetment – Excavation – 130 ft duck boarding laid – 100 men on trench mortar emplacements	B37+28SW U.15 c.3.3
21 & 16 4 hrs 3/4 25.7.16 ONLY WAY	Deepening & widening trench – Carrying material – Night quiet	B37+28SW V.14 c.5.2
6 G 2 John 25.7.16 ONTARIO AVP & LOOP	Wiring & fixing frames – Digging trench – Sandbag revetment – Having break – Zero point	B37+28SW V.14 c.2.14
7 E 13 John 25.7.16 LOWNDES AV MJELARABSOQUEFM	Fixing frames – Wire netting trailing entrance – Trench shaft – Machinegun for A.E. post C. in LOWNDES AV – Work completed at FARM – Being night 20 shovels & picks 6 rakes & wrens blown up by shell in LAV.	B37+28SW U.26 c.2.7
7 C 8C 12 thus 25.7.16 ONLY WAY	Revetting – Laying duck boards – Cutting entrance of tunnel – Carrying material – Hostile enemy shell fire	B37+28SW V.14 c.5.2
8 G 14hrs 25.7.16 TORONTO AV HILL 63	Fixing frames – C. war – sandbag revetment – Laying duck boards – Excavation – Carrying material – Heavy shell fire – Casualties – 1 O.R. wounded	B37+28SW V.15 c.3.3
21 G 4 hrs 15 to 26.7.16 ONLY WAY	Deepening & widening trench – Building up	B37+28SW V.14 c.5.2

Army Form C. 2118.

WAR DIARY
or
INTELLIGENCE SUMMARY.
(Erase heading not required.)

Instructions regarding War Diaries and Intelligence Summaries are contained in F.S. Regs., Part II and the Staff Manual respectively. Title pages will be prepared in manuscript.

Hour, Date, Place			Summary of Events and Information	Remarks and references to Appendices
8 to 10 hrs	27.7.16	ONTARIO AVE LOOP	Wiring & fixing frames – Digging out trench – Laying Duck Boards – Can't dig westward – 12 cattle fires –	BT 7 2 SSW U14 C 2.4
7.30 15 hrs	27.7.16	LOWNDES AV	Returning trench – laying duck boards –	BT 7 2 SSW U28 a b c
14 to 19 hrs	27.7.16	ONLY WAY	Entrance to trench completed – Nothing of packing entrance	BT 7 2 SSW U14 C 5...
8 to 14 hrs	27.7.16	TORONTO AV #4.4.13	Fixing Trench O Dug out frames – 40 yds westwards – 20 yds dug out frame – Laying	BT 7 2 SSW U14 C 5...
21.7.16 27 & 2 hrs 27.7.16		ONLY WAY	Duck boards – Excavation – Cleaning – Deepening & widening trench – Carrying material – Gas alarm at	BT 7 2 SSW U14 C 5-2
8 to 10 hrs	28.7.16	ONTARIO AV Y LOOP	Wiring & fixing frames – Duck boards – Drainage & cattle - exits –	BT 7 2 SSW U14 C 2.4
7.30 to 16 hrs	28.7.16	LOWNDES AV & FEENAN'S BREAKWATER	Fixing frames – Laying duck boards – Nothing – Drainage – Entrance to dugout	BT 7 2 SSW U28 a b c
14 to 19 hrs	28.7.16	ONLY WAY	Main entrance of trench completed – 40 yds duck boards –	BT 7 2 SSW U14 C 5,2
14 hrs	28.9.16	TORONTO AV & L.13	30 yds frames – Digging dug out frames – Revetting – Raising & widening pickets – Duck boards –	BT 7 2 SSW U14 C 3,2
6-30 hrs 16 hrs 13 hrs – 14 hrs	30.7.16 30.7.16 30.7.16 30.7.16	ONTARIO AVE LOWNDES AVE REGENT ST TORONTO AV	Dumu lts, wiring duck boards Fixing frames – Laying shell boards. Digging communication Trenches – Fixing frames – Laying duck boards –	28 S.W. U14 d 4,4. 28 S.W. U26 a 28 S.W. U14 c 4 28 S.W. U14 c 3,3
6-30 hrs 15 hrs 13 hrs – 14 hrs	31.7.16 31.7.16 31.7.16 31.7.16	ONTARIO AVE LOWNDES AV REGENT ST TORONTO AVE	Building duck boards – Laying sandbags Fixing frames – Laying shell boards – Drainage – Nothing Digging communication trenches – Fixing frames – Laying duck boards	28 S.W. U14 d 4,4. 28 S.W. U26 a 28 S.W. U14 c 4 28 S.W. U14 c 3,3

A.J. ???, LT. COLONEL
COMMANDING 19TH (S) BN
MIDDLESEX REGT (P.W.O.)

19th / 1/5/ R. Middlesex Regt (Pioneers)

Army Form C. 2118.

Vol 4

WAR DIARY
or
INTELLIGENCE SUMMARY.
(Erase heading not required.)

Instructions regarding War Diaries and Intelligence Summaries are contained in F.S. Regs., Part II. and the Staff Manual respectively. Title pages will be prepared in manuscript.

Hour, Date, Place		Summary of Events and Information	Remarks and references to Appendices
6½-20 hr.	5-8-16 Ontario Rn.	Continuing earthworks, referencing drainage caused by hostile shell fire.	28 S.W. O. 19 d. 1.4. AAA
8-14 hr.	5-8-16 Swansdowne Ave.	Burying deadwounds during previous.	28.S.W. O.26 b.49. AAA
8-19 hr.	5-8-16 Regent St	Very little work done owing to continuous shellfire, everyone returned.	28.S. W. O.21c.2.6. AAA
8-14 hr.	5-8-16 Toronto Rn.	63 trench frames fixed, 70 yds of earth excavated, 3 dug outs commenced.	28.S. W. O.15 c.3.3. AAA
6½-20 hr.	6-8-16 Ontario Rn.	Continuing earthworks and trying excellence.	28 S.W. J.14 d.4.4. AAA
8-14 hr.	6-8-16 Swansdowne Ave.	54 frames fixed. Brushwood continued.	28 S.W. O.26 b.4.9. AAA
6-8-16	Regent St	Completing drain, lentaining.	28.S. W. O.21 c.3.6. AAA
6-8-16	Toronto Ave.	38 ft. dug out completed, 23 frames fixed, 1.80 cubic feet of earth excavated, 3 dug outs developed, 3 dug into flanked. No work today owing to bombardery & withdrawal of original batt. installation force.	28.S. W. O.15 c.3.3. AAA
7-8-16	—		

(73989) W4141—463. 400,000. 9/14. H.&J.Ltd. Forms/C. 2118/10.

Army Form C. 2118.

WAR DIARY
or
INTELLIGENCE SUMMARY.
(Erase heading not required.)

Instructions regarding War Diaries and Intelligence Summaries are contained in F.S. Regs., Part II and the Staff Manual respectively. Title pages will be prepared in manuscript.

Hour, Date, Place		Summary of Events and Information	Remarks and references to Appendices
4½-20h.r.	7-8-16 Ontario lines.	Bombing sections to digging learner pits and completing entrenchers	28 S.W.U 14 d. 1. 4. AM
8-14h.r.	8-8-16 Brandon lines	54 hours field drill & wands continued	28 S.W.U 26 d. 4. 8. AM
14 in 19	9-8-16 Dugout H.Q.	Company instructs making trenches and continuing	28 S.W.U 21 d. 8. 3 AM
14 in	9-8-16 Toronto lines	½ Trench mortar fired 50 rounds of H.E. at front line 2, raid on dugouts & front line 3, others extinguished	28 S.W.U 27 d. 6. 3. AM
9-1-8-7		Front Bay Battery for ½ hour afterwards	
1-20h.r.	10-8-16 Ontario lines	Revetting and completing entrenchers	28 S.W.U 14 d. 4. 4.
14 in	10-8-16 Brandon lines	Work on trenches continued, trenches from firing line to communication continued	28 S.W.U 26 d. 4. 8.
14 in	10-8-16 Dugout H.Q.	Cutting up continued	28 S.W.U 21 d. 2. 9.
14 in	10-8-16 Toronto lines	24 men assembled at Brigade front to procure fund	28 S.W.U 15 d. 3. 3.

(73989) W4141-463. 400,000. 9/14. H. & J. Ltd. Forms/C. 2118/10.

Army Form C. 2118.

WAR DIARY
or
INTELLIGENCE SUMMARY

(Erase heading not required.)

Instructions regarding War Diaries and Intelligence Summaries are contained in F. S. Regs., Part II. and the Staff Manual respectively. Title Pages will be prepared in manuscript.

Place	Date	Hour	Summary of Events and Information	Remarks and references to Appendices
Ontario Ave.	11-8-16	8-14hr	Bivouac fits and earthworks	28 S W V114 d.4.9
Lucknow Ave.	11-8-16	8-14hr	Bushwhacking, entrance to Ail preats completed.	28 S W V 226 b.4.8
Toronto Ave.	11-8-16	8-19hr	149 Trench improved, 14 Dugout [?] down loaded 480 sandbags filled, 55 40 ft [?]	28 S W V137 c.3.3
Royal St	11-8-16	8-14hr	Revetting + cutting up.	28 S W V21 c.3. 9.3.
Ontario Ave	12-8-16	8-14 hr	Bivouac fits & earthworks	28 S W V144 d.2.4
Lucknow Ave.	12-8-16	8-14hr	Little work done owing to hostile situation. 14 prisoners food	28 S W V c.9.48
	12-8-16	8-19hr	buying dustslworks, filling in funnel	
Royal St	12-8-16	8-19hr	889 ft of dustslworks laid 2 [?] prisoners found [?] moved found	28 S W V15 c.3.3
Toronto Ave	12-8-16	8-19hr		28 S W V21 c.3.6
	13-8-16	—	Rest Day. Battering Parade.	

2449 Wt. W4957/Mg0 750,000 1/16 J.B.C. & A. Forms/C.2118/12.

Army Form C. 2118.

WAR DIARY
or
INTELLIGENCE SUMMARY
(Erase heading not required.)

Instructions regarding War Diaries and Intelligence Summaries are contained in F.S. Regs., Part II. and the Staff Manual respectively. Title Pages will be prepared in manuscript.

Place	Date	Hour	Summary of Events and Information	Remarks and references to Appendices
Ontario Line	14-8-16	6-2h	Enthusiasm continued	S.S. S.14.d 2.4
Kirchner Line	14-8-16	8-14h	Enemy distributed 150 prisoners	S.S. S.14.b 4.5
Regent St	14-8-16	8-20h	Enemy material, machine gun ammunition, etc.	S.S. S.21 c.7.3
Toronto Line	14-8-16	8-14h	7 prisoners fired 180 rounds on fired gun	C.3 S.11.b.9
Onslow	15-8-16	6	No works doing to include rifle	
Onslow	16-8-16		Cultivating trenches and enemy options of enemy battalion round	
Onslow	17-8-16		Relieved by 1st Bn. South Staffords marched to the carpe Tranen area	S.24 A.3
S.36 A.3	18-8-16	9-	Company Training Bathing	S.36 A.3

WAR DIARY
or
INTELLIGENCE SUMMARY

Army Form C. 2118.

Place	Date	Hour	Summary of Events and Information	Remarks and references to Appendices
S 36 A 3	19-8-16	8-14 h	Battalion Training	S.36.A.3.
S 36 A 3	20-8-16	8-14 h	Battalion Training	S.36 A 3
S 36 A 3	21-8-16	8-14 h	Battalion Training	S.36 A.3
S 36 A 3	22-8-16	8-14 h	Battalion Training	S.36 A.3
S 36 A 3	23-8-16	8-14 h	Battalion Training	S.36 A.3
S 36 A 3	24-8-16	26 Nov	Battalion entrained for Pont Remy, billeted at Aully & Huts shelter for Officers	
S 36 A 3	25-8-16	8-14 h	Rest, moved to Coequencel and moved by lorry	
Aully	26-8-16	8-14 h	Battalion Training	
Aully	27-8-16	8-14 h	Battalion Training	
Aully	28-8-16	8-14 h	Battalion inspected by G.O.C 43rd Division	
Aully	29-8-16	8-14 h	Battalion took part in scheme for training of R.A.M.C.	
Aully	30-8-16	8-14 h	Battalion Training	
Aully	31-8-16	8-14 h	Battalion Training	

A. Horn.
Commanding 19/8/16 1/9 Gr Yorkshire

Army Form C. 2118.

WAR DIARY
or
INTELLIGENCE SUMMARY

(Erase heading not required.)

September, 1916.

Vol 5

Place	Date	Hour	Summary of Events and Information	Remarks and references to Appendices
Adty & Huts Dublin	1-9-16	9-5	Battalion Training.	
Adty & Huts Dublin	2-9-16	9-5pm	Battalion Training.	
Adty to Huts Dublin	3-9-16	—	Battalion move to XVth Corps Reserve — Empty trenches 8 & 9 F.9	
F.9.	4-9-16	—	Rest Day	
Milh Avenue A" coy	5-9-16	5.30am 3pm	Digging communication Trench. Hemp of revealed but given 576 - 516682	
Fleur Ave B" coy	5-9-16	5.30am 3pm	Digging communication Trench. 4.5.70.19 as noted.	
J. Aw. F Days	6-9-16	5.30am 3pm	Continuation of communication Trench — 12 men # wounded	

Army Form C. 2118.

WAR DIARY
or
INTELLIGENCE SUMMARY
(Erase heading not required.)

Instructions regarding War Diaries and Intelligence Summaries are contained in F. S. Regs., Part II. and the Staff Manual respectively. Title Pages will be prepared in manuscript.

Place	Date	Hour	Summary of Events and Information	Remarks and references to Appendices
Flanders	6.9.16	5.30am – 3pm	Continuation of communication Trench – 115 off excavated.	
Ditto emp.				
ditto	7.9.16	5.30am – 3pm	150 yards of Trench widened & deepened.	
A & B emp.				
Flanders	7.9.16		150 yards of Trench dug to average of 4 ft in depth	
Ditto		6-9.30pm		
ditto				
ditto				
H & D emp. Ox	8.9.16	5.30am – 3pm	9 yards of Trench dug and deepened	
Flanders				
B emp.	8.9.16	5.30pm – 8pm	80 off 5 with excavated trench widened to 4 ft	
ditto				
ditto	9.9.16	5.30am – 3pm	Good progress made although heavily shelled.	
A & B Emp	9.9.16			
Flanders				
Ditto emp	9.9.16	5.30pm – 8pm	100 ft of earth excavated – 150 yds deepened to 4'.6"	

2449 Wt. W14957/M90 750,000 1/16 J.B.C. & A. Forms/C.2118/12.

Army Form C. 2118.

WAR DIARY
or
INTELLIGENCE SUMMARY

(Erase heading not required.)

Instructions regarding War Diaries and Intelligence Summaries are contained in F. S. Regs., Part II. and the Staff Manual respectively. Title Pages will be prepared in manuscript.

Place	Date	Hour	Summary of Events and Information	Remarks and references to Appendices
High Wood A & D Coy	10-9-16	4.30am 3am	Continuation of communication Trench to Chimney Walk –	
Flers Line B & C Coy	10-9-16	4.30am 3am	main ground stunt on continuation of Flers line – 60 yds completed	
High Wood A & D Coy	11-9-16	7pm 3am	170 yds of trench widened & levelled, 6,6000 ft of duck boards recovered	
Flers Line B & C	11-9-16	7pm 3am	Trench continued through Debrill Wood, connection made with chimney line	
High Wood A & D	12-9-16	7pm 3am	150 yds of shellsounding line – 600 ft of cable evacuated	
Flers Line B & C	12-9-16	7pm 3am	Work consisted of connecting of shell holes in Debrill Wood	
High Wood A & D	13-9-16	7pm 3am	400 yds of shellwound found	
Flers Line B & C	13-9-16	7pm 3am	Connection of shell holes completed	
Fricourt	14-9-16	—	Rest Day	

WAR DIARY
or
INTELLIGENCE SUMMARY

(Erase heading not required.)

Army Form C. 2118.

Instructions regarding War Diaries and Intelligence Summaries are contained in F. S. Regs., Part II and the Staff Manual respectively. Title Pages will be prepared in manuscript.

Place	Date	Hour	Summary of Events and Information	Remarks and references to Appendices
Green Dump from Quarry E.17.A.7.8 to A9 Dugs	15-9-16	6 a.m – 5 p.m	Road repaired and made good for traffic widened to 15 ft	
Huntingdon Rd	15-9-16	6 a.m – 6 p.m	Trench from Gordon Rd to Longueval widened for 150 yds and wired away to make road 18 ft wide	
Picc. cup Gunpit Rd	16-9-16	6 a.m – 9 p.m	Road widened to 18 ft	
A9 D. coy Huntingdon Rd	16-9-16	6 a.m – 6 p.m	Road levelled to Delville Wood and widened to 18 ft	
B4 coy		6 p.m	Battalion returned to Fricourt camp	
Longueval	17-9-16 2 p.m		Evacuated 12 noon, to well-known field tunnel	
Fricourt Tunnel to Sudall Lines	18-9-16	6 a.m – 4 p.m		
Sudall Tunnel ? to Sudall Lines	19-9-16	6 a.m – 3 p.m	Tunnel dug to 7 ft throughout entire length	

Army Form C. 2118.

WAR DIARY
or
INTELLIGENCE SUMMARY
(Erase heading not required.)

Instructions regarding War Diaries and Intelligence Summaries are contained in F. S. Regs., Part II. and the Staff Manual respectively. Title Pages will be prepared in manuscript.

Place	Date	Hour	Summary of Events and Information	Remarks and references to Appendices
yeah Trunk to Switch line	20.4.16	6 a.m to 3 p.m	Completed cable Trunk to depth of 3½ ft and 2½ ft wide at bottom & 2½ ft wide at top.	
yeah Trunk to Switch line	21.4.16	6 a.m to 3 p.m	Laid in division and tape covered, completed trenching.	
yeah Trunk to Switch line	22.4.16	6 a.m to 3 p.m	Carrying tonduits for trenching - completed trenching.	
Forward camp	23.4.16	—	Battalion in Rest.	
Forward camp	24.4.16	—	Battalion in Rest.	
Forward camp	25.4.16	—	Battalion in Rest.	

2449 Wt. W14957/M90 750,000 1/16 J.B.C. & A. Forms/C.2118/12.

Army Form C. 2118.

WAR DIARY
or
INTELLIGENCE SUMMARY

(Erase heading not required.)

Instructions regarding War Diaries and Intelligence Summaries are contained in F. S. Regs., Part II. and the Staff Manual respectively. Title Pages will be prepared in manuscript.

Place	Date	Hour	Summary of Events and Information	Remarks and references to Appendices
Forward trench	26.9.16	—	Battalion in work	
Forward trench	27.9.16	—	Battalion in rest	
Forward trench	28.9.16	—	One company proceeded to trench extension attached to 21st Division	
Forward trench	29.9.16	8.15 am to 6 am	Wiring in front of trench 100 ft wire - 400 yds of front wire put out	57 c.S.W 26.9.13
Forward trench	30.9.16	8.15 pm to 6 am	250 yds trench dug 3'6" ft deep. Revetted throughout.	57 c.S.W 26.9.13

A. Hume
LT. COLONEL,
COMMANDING 19TH (S) BN.
MIDDLESEX REGT. (PIONEERS.)

2449 Wt. W14957/M90 750,000 1/16 J.B.C. & A. Forms/C.2118/12.

Army Form C. 2118.

41 Div / Vol 6

WAR DIARY
or
INTELLIGENCE SUMMARY
(Erase heading not required.)

Instructions regarding War Diaries and Intelligence Summaries are contained in F. S. Regs., Part II. and the Staff Manual respectively. Title Pages will be prepared in manuscript.

Place	Date	Hour	Summary of Events and Information	Remarks and references to Appendices
Cuddle Trench	1-10-16	6 a.m.	2400 yards of trench dug to an average depth of 3'6".	
		2 p.m.		
Cuddle Trench	2-10-16	6 a.m.	1200 yards of trench completed to width of 7 ft.	
		2 p.m.		
Cuddle Trench	3-10-16	6 a.m.	Owing to heavy rain work greatly hindered. Still 1200 yards however got into trench from South Trench on Northerly direction Bn. 6 ft. 600 yards from South Trench completed.	
		2 p.m.		
A.B.C.Coys Red Lane Reserve Line	4-10-16	6 a.m.	Continuous wet night. Parapets of trench disturbed in 4 ft and slush.	
		4 p.m.		
D Coy in Observation Post	4-10-16	6 a.m.	Getting forward supplies of rations from Supply dump.	
		2 p.m.		
Res't from Reserve Line A.B.C.	5-10-16	6 a.m.	Had very unpleasant journey descending slope from Front Line then stumbling through	
		8 p.m.		
		4 a.m.	the slush in the trench.	
D Coy in Observation Post	5-10-16	6 a.m.	2 O.P.'s opened up. Observation good. No firing today 30 prisoners deserted.	
		2 p.m.		

2449 Wt. W14957/M90 750,000 1/16 J.B.C. & A. Forms/C.2118/12.

WAR DIARY
or
INTELLIGENCE SUMMARY

(Erase heading not required.)

Army Form C. 2118.

Instructions regarding War Diaries and Intelligence Summaries are contained in F.S. Regs., Part II. and the Staff Manual respectively. Title Pages will be prepared in manuscript.

Place	Date	Hour	Summary of Events and Information	Remarks and references to Appendices
Fish Alley A	5.10.16	8 p.m.	two yards of trench bombed and cleared	
Spure Alley B	6.10.16	4 a.m. 8 p.m. 4 a.m.	completely cleared and consolidated	
Pioneer Lane C	6.10.16	8 p.m.	2 m² yards of trench dug to a depth of 6 feet	
Observation Post D	6.10.16	6 a.m. — 2 p.m.	50 yards and 50 firebays cleared from spare point – Bombing completed	
Fosse Alley	7.10.16	8 p.m. 4 a.m.	continues attached to Brigade Headquarters for work on C.T. – 5 guides kept out to shew new division of trenches	
Technique & Pioneer Lane	8.10.16	8 p.m. 4 a.m.	Some yards of trench from front line dug to depth of 4'6" & 3'6".	
Tech Tosse Pioneer Lane	9.10.16	8 p.m. 4 a.m.	The intensity of trench checked by orders of 141st Infantry Brigade commander	
Test Lane Spare Alley	10.10.16	6 a.m. — 12 noon	Particulars of issued for a length of two yards of trench newly – cleared of	
Huddleston	11.10.16	—	Battalion in rest	

WAR DIARY
or
INTELLIGENCE SUMMARY

(Erase heading not required.)

Army Form C. 2118.

Place	Date	Hour	Summary of Events and Information	Remarks and references to Appendices
[Montauban]	12.10.16	4 pm	Battalion relieved by 11th Batt. Lancashire Regt.	
Montauban	13.10.16	8 am to 4 pm.	Battalion repairing road BERNAFAY – LONGUEVAL.	
Montauban	14.10.16	8 am to 4 pm.	Battalion repairing road BERNAFAY – LONGUEVAL.	
Montauban	15.10.16	8 am to 12 noon.	Battalion repairing road BERNAFAY – LONGUEVAL.	
BUIRE.	16.10.16	6:30 am	Batt. marched to BUIRE.	
Buire			Transport by road to HALLENCOURT.	
Hallencourt	17.10.16		Batt. entrained by two trains for DISEMENT. R.O.Y.	
Hallencourt	18.10.16	8 am.	Batt. arrived at HALLENCOURT. – R.O.Y.	
Hallencourt	19.10.16		Rest.	
Hallencourt	20.10.16	7.0 pm	Batt. entrained at LONGPRÉ for CAESTRE.	
Rouge Croix	21.10.16	6 am	Batt. arrived at CAESTRE and marched to ROUGE CROIX.	
Rouge Croix	22.10.16	10. am.	Batt. marched to BERTHEN.	
BERTHEN.	23.10.16	10 am.	Batt. marches to MICMAC CAMP near DICKEBUSCH and relieved 4th Australian Pioneers.	
MICMAC Camp	24.10.16		Officers viewed trenches	
MICMAC Camp.	25.10.16	7 to 15.00	Cutting channels under duckboards for drainage. Old Kent Rd. Shelley Lane. Convent Lane. Voormezeele Switch. – C.T's.	
		8 am.	Three Companies bathing.	
MICMAC	26.10/16	8:30 am to 5 pm.	Four Companies clearing, draining, duckboarding, revetting & cleaning C.T's. Shelley Lane, Catacomb Lane, Old Kent Road, Chilley Lane, Spionkoft Lane, Queen Victoria St. Shelter St. Voormezeele Gdn. Poppy Lane.	

4

Army Form C. 2118.

WAR DIARY
or
INTELLIGENCE SUMMARY

(Erase heading not required.)

Instructions regarding War Diaries and Intelligence Summaries are contained in F. S. Regs., Part II. and the Staff Manual respectively. Title Pages will be prepared in manuscript.

Place	Date	Hour	Summary of Events and Information	Remarks and references to Appendices
MICMAC Camp	28/10/16	7am to 5pm	Four Companies patrolling, general repairs, carrying material, sandbagging, duckboarding, revetting, draining Shelley Lane, Rutherland Lane, Old Kent Road, Forward Lane, Chester Lane, Rd Trench, Queen Victoria St, Oxford St, Oaster Lane, Voormezeele Switch, Poppy Lane.	
		9am-5pm	Building covered standings for horses.	
MICMAC Camp	29/10/16	7am-3pm	Four Coys patrolling, general repairs, sandbagging, duckboarding, revetting, draining Shelley Lane, Satinwood Lane, Old Kent Rd, Forward Lane, Chester Lane, P.O. Trench, Queen Victoria St, Oxford St, Oaster Lane, Voormezeele Switch, Middlesex Lane, Elsenwalle St, Poppy Lane. Carrying materials by night to forward area.	
		9am-5pm	Building covered standings for horses. Work delayed owing to lack of material.	
MICMAC Camp	29/10/16	7am to 5pm	Four Coys patrolling, general repairs and maintenance of all C.T.'s in Bril area.	
		9am to 5pm	Building covered standings for horses.	
MICMAC Camp	30/10/16	7am to 5pm	Four Coys patrolling, general repairs and maintenance of all C.T.'s in Bril area.	
		9am-5pm	Building covered standings for horses.	
MICMAC Camp	31/10/16	7am to 5pm	Four Coys patrolling, general repairs and maintenance of all C.T.'s in Bril area.	
		9am to 5pm	Building covered standings for horses.	

A Wilson, Lieut. Col.
Comdg 19th Middlesex Rgt Pioneers

From :- Officer Commanding,
       19th (S) Battalion
       Middlesex Regt.(Pioneers.)

To   :- Headquarters,
        41st Division, A.

              Attached please find War Diary

for November, 1916.

                                Lt. Colonel,
                         Commanding 19th (S) B'n
                         Middlesex Regt.(Pioneers.)

December 1st 1916.

No. 296.

Army Form C. 2118.

WAR DIARY
or
INTELLIGENCE SUMMARY
(Erase heading not required.)

1/1st I.D. 146 (1st West Riding) (Durham)

Vol 7

Place	Date	Hour	Summary of Events and Information	Remarks and references to Appendices
Micmac Camp	1/11/16		Battn rest day & Bathing.	
Micmac Camp	2/11/16	7am to 5pm	Four Coys general repairs on all C.T's in Divisional area.	
		9am to 5pm	Building covered standings for horses & drawing bricks from YPRES.	
Micmac Camp	3/11/16	7am to 5pm	Four Coys general repairs to all C.T's in Divisional area	
		9am to 5pm	Building covered standings for horses & drawing bricks from YPRES.	
	4/11/16	7am to 5pm	Four companies general repairs to all C.T's in Divisional area.	
		9am to 5pm	Building covered standings for horses & drawing bricks from YPRES	
	5/11/16	7am to 5pm	Four companies general repairs to all C.T's in Divisional Area. POPPY LANE C.T. Has damaged in many places also OLD KENT ROAD C.T. part of which repaired in POPPY LANE was blown in by T.M. Bomb.	
		9am to 5pm	Building covered standings for horses & drawing bricks from YPRES.	
	6/11/16	7am to 5pm	Four companies finished repair to all C.T's in Divisional Area being & general renewal of revetments in many places has taken place in the French front & othersside the Trenches	
		9am to 5pm	Building covered standings for horses & drawing bricks from Ypres	

Army Form C. 2118.

WAR DIARY
or
INTELLIGENCE SUMMARY
(Erase heading not required.)

Instructions regarding War Diaries and Intelligence Summaries are contained in F. S. Regs., Part II. and the Staff Manual respectively. Title Pages will be prepared in manuscript.

Place	Date	Hour	Summary of Events and Information	Remarks and references to Appendices
MENIN ROAD	1/4/16	7am to 8am	Four companies General Repair to all trenches in Divisional area. Owing to heavy shelling No calls in Jan-May the whole trench are not in use any more the trench was used in	
		9am to 5pm	Building covered standings for horses & drawing fuel from YPRES.	
	8/4/16	7am to 5pm	Battalion Rest day. Patrols made out to reconnoitre for any way to get the trench CONVENT KANE TRENCH was taken in for field of fire hole	
	9/4/16	7am to 5pm	General repairs to all C.T's in the Divisional area. Owing to heavy rain no work was done in the trenches, the morning parties having to repair damage due to the rains in the trenches	
		4pm to 5pm	Building covered standings for horses & drawing fuel from YPRES	
	10/4/16	8 to 9am	General repairs to all C.T's in Divisional area	
		9am	Building covered standings for horses	
	11/4/16	8am to 9pm	General repairs to C.T.O	
		3am to 8am	Building covered standings for horses	
	12/4/16	8am to 6pm	General repairs to C.T's	
		7am to 11pm	Building covered standings for horses	
	13/4/16		General repairs to C.T.O	
		7am to 4pm	Building Covered Standings for horses	

WAR DIARY or INTELLIGENCE SUMMARY

Army Form C. 2118.

Place	Date	Hour	Summary of Events and Information	Remarks and references to Appendices
MIC MAC Camp	14/11/16		Battalion rest day - Church Services & Bathing.	
	15/11/16	9am-4pm	General repairs to C.T's.	
	16/11/16	9am-4pm	Building covered standings for horses. General repairs to C.T's.	
	17/11/16	9am-4pm	Building covered standings for horses. General repairs to C.T's.	
	18/11/16	9am-4pm	Building covered standings for horses. General repairs & C.T's.	
	19/11/16	9am-4pm	Building covered standings for horses. General repairs & maintenance of C.T's.	
	19/11/16	9am-4pm	General repairs & maintenance of C.T's. Building covered standings for horses.	
	20/11/16	8am-4pm	General repairs to C.T's. Building French Mortar Emplacements. Duckboard walks.	
	21/11/16		Building Covered standings for horses. Rest day. Church Services & Bathing.	
	22/11/16	9am-4pm	Building French Mortar Emplacements. Patrolling C.T's.	
	22/11/16	9am-4pm	General repairs & maintenance of C.T's. Building French Mortar Emplacements. Building Covered standings for horses.	
	23/11/16	9am-4pm	General repairs and maintenance of C.T's. Building French Mortar Emplacements. Building covered standings for horses.	

Army Form C. 2118.

WAR DIARY
or
INTELLIGENCE SUMMARY

(Erase heading not required.)

Instructions regarding War Diaries and Intelligence Summaries are contained in F. S. Regs., Part II. and the Staff Manual respectively. Title Pages will be prepared in manuscript.

Place	Date	Hour	Summary of Events and Information	Remarks and references to Appendices
Mieurs Camp	24/11/16		General repairs & maintenance of C.T's. Building T.M. Emplacements. Building covered standings for horses.	
	25/11/16	8am-4pm	General repairs to C.T's. Building T.M. Emplacements. Building covered standings for horses.	
	26/11/16	8am-4pm	General repairs & maintenance of C.T's. Building covered standings for horses.	
	27/11/16	7am-4pm	Building covered standings T.M. Emplacements.	
	28/11/16	8am-4pm	General repairs & patrolling C.T's. Building T.M. Emplacements. Building covered standings for horses.	
	29/11/16		Rest day. Bathing. Patrolling C.T's.	
			General repairs & patrolling, wiring C.T's. Building T.M. Emplacements. Building covered standings for horses.	
	30/11/16	8am-4pm	General repairs, wiring to C.T's. Building T.M. Emplacements. Building covered standings for horses.	
		6am-4pm	Building covered standings for horses.	

A.I. Turno LT. COLONEL.
COMMANDING 19TH (S) BN.
MIDDLESEX REGT. (PIONEERS)

Army Form C. 2118.

WAR DIARY
or
INTELLIGENCE SUMMARY

(Erase heading not required.)

10th A.I.B. .... Vol 8

Instructions regarding War Diaries and Intelligence Summaries are contained in F. S. Regs., Part II. and the Staff Manual respectively. Title Pages will be prepared in manuscript.

Place	Date	Hour	Summary of Events and Information	Remarks and references to Appendices
Mennes Camp	1/12/16		General repairs to C.T's. Building T.M. Emplacements & Horse Standings	
	2/12/16		do	
	3/12/16		do	
	4/12/16		do	
	5/12/16		Battn rest day & bathing	
	6/12/16		General repairs & wiring C.T's Building T.M. Emplacements & Horse Standings	
	7/12/16		do	
	8/12/16		do	
	9/12/16		do	
	10/12/16		do	
	11/12/16		Battn rest day & bathing	
	12/12/16		General repairs, wiring work on C.T's, T.M Emplacements & Horse Standings	
	13/12/16		do	
	14/12/16		do	
	15/12/16		do	
	16/12/16		do	
	17/12/16		do	
	18/12/16		Battn rest day & bathing	
	19/12/16		General work wiring C.T's. Bomb Stores & Horse Standings. D Coy attached to Corps for work on Corps Light Railways	
	20/12/16		General work wiring C.T's. Building Bomb Stores & Horse Standings	
	21/12/16		General work wiring C.T's. Building Horse Standings	
	22/12/16		do	
	23/12/16		do	

2449 Wt. W14957/M90 750,000 1/16 J.B.C. & A. Forms/C.2118/12.

WAR DIARY
or
INTELLIGENCE SUMMARY

Army Form C. 2118.

Place	Date	Hour	Summary of Events and Information	Remarks and references to Appendices
Minnes Camp	24/12/16		General work on C.T's. Building Horse Standings.	
	25/12/16		Church Services. Working parties sent out every ¼ to trenches being damaged.	
	26/12/16		General work on C.T's. Pushing road to stables.	
	27/12/16		ditto	
	28/12/16		Battery Patrols on C.T's. Building Horse Standings.	
	29/12/16		General work on C.T's. Building Horse Standings.	
	30/12/16		ditto	
	31/12/16		ditto	

G Watson Major
Commanding 14th M.G.C.
(Middlesex Regt. Pioneers)

From :- Officer Commanding
        19th (S) Battalion
        Middlesex Regt. (Pioneers.)

To :- Headquarters,
      41st Division, A.

Herewith War Diary for January 1917.

                                    Lt. Col.
                        Commanding 19th (S) B'n
                        Middlesex Regt. (Pioneers.)

No. 450.

February 1st 1917.

Army Form C. 2118.

WAR DIARY
or
INTELLIGENCE SUMMARY 19th Bn Middlesex Regt (Pioneers)
(Erase heading not required.)

Vol 9

Instructions regarding War Diaries and Intelligence Summaries are contained in F. S. Regs, Part II. and the Staff Manual respectively. Title Pages will be prepared in manuscript.

Place	Date	Hour	Summary of Events and Information	Remarks and references to Appendices
Mieaux Camp	1/1/17		General work on C.T's, duckwalks.	
	2/1/17		Bathing a rest day - trenches patrolled.	
	3/1/17		General work on C.T's.	
	4/1/17		do	
	5/1/17		do	
	6/1/17		do	
	7/1/17		do	
	8/1/17		do	
	9/1/17		Bathing + rest day. trenches patrolled.	
	10/1/17		General work on C.T's.	
	11/1/17		do	
	12/1/17		B & C Coys moved from Mieaux Camp to walled enclosure at Dickebusch. A Company moved from Mieaux Camp to Mieaux Lauts from Dickebusch huts.	
	13/1/17		General work on C.T's.	
	14/1/17		do	
	15/1/17		do	
	16/1/17		Rest day + bathing. Trenches patrolled.	
	17/1/17		General work on C.T's	
	18/1/17		do	
	19/1/17		do	
	20/1/17		do	
	21/1/17		do	

Army Form C. 2118.

WAR DIARY
or
INTELLIGENCE SUMMARY

(Erase heading not required.)

19th Bn Middlesex Regt (Pioneers)

Instructions regarding War Diaries and Intelligence Summaries are contained in F. S. Regs., Part II. and the Staff Manual respectively. Title Pages will be prepared in manuscript.

Place	Date	Hour	Summary of Events and Information	Remarks and references to Appendices
Meurice Camp	23/1/17		General work on C.T's	
	24/1/17		do.	
	24/1/17		do	
	25/1/17		Battn rest day & bathing	
	26/1/17		General work on C.T's	
	27/1/17		do	
	28/1/17		do	
	29/1/17		Battn rest day & bathing	
	30/1/17		General work on C.T's	
	31/1/17			

A. Hume
LT. COLONEL,
COMMANDING 19TH (S) BN.
MIDDLESEX REGT. (PIONEERS.)

From :- Officer Commanding
       19th (S) Battalion
       Middlesex Regt.(Pioneers.)

To :- Headquarters,
      41st Division, A.

Herewith War Diary for the month of February 1917.

                                A.H.Lewis   Lt. Col.
                           Commanding 19th (S) B'n
                           Middlesex Regt.(Pioneers.)

No.507.

March 1st 1917.

Army Form C. 2118.

WAR DIARY
or
INTELLIGENCE SUMMARY 19th Bn Middlesex Regt (Pioneers)

(Erase heading not required.)

Vol. 10

Place	Date	Hour	Summary of Events and Information	Remarks and references to Appendices
Micmac Camp	1/2/17		General work on C.T's	
	2/2/17		do	
	3/2/17		do	
	4/2/17		do	
	5/2/17		do	
	6/2/17		Rest day & bathing	
	7/2/17		General work on C.T's	
	8/2/17		do	
	9/2/17		do	
	10/2/17		do	
	11/2/17		do	
	12/2/17		do	
	13/2/17		Rest day & bathing	
	14/2/17		General work on C.T's	
	15/2/17		do	
	16/2/17		do	
	17/2/17		do	
	18/2/17		do	
	19/2/17		Rest day & bathing. Working parties out QUEEN VICTORIA ST & POPPY LANE.	
	20/2/17		General work on C.T's	
	21/2/17		do	
	22/2/17		do	
	23/2/17		do	
	24/2/17		do	
	25/2/17		do	
	26/2/17		Rest day & bathing	
	27/2/17		do do	
	28/2/17		General work on C.T's	

A. Hume LT. COLONEL.
COMMANDING 19TH (S) BN.
MIDDLESEX REGT. (PIONEERS.)

Confidential

War Diary

of

19th Bn. Middlesex Regt.

(Pioneers)

For month of March 1917

From :- Officer Commanding
       19th (S) Battalion
       Middlesex Regt.(Pioneers.)

To   :- Headquarters,
        41st Division, A.

            Herewith War Diary for the

month of March 1917.

                              A. Humes Lt. Col.
                        Commanding 19th (S) B'n
                         Middlesex Regt.(Pioneers.)

No. 581.

March 31st 1917.

Army Form C. 2118.

WAR DIARY
or
INTELLIGENCE SUMMARY 19th Bn Middlesex Regt (Pioneers)

(Erase heading not required.)

Place	Date	Hour	Summary of Events and Information	Remarks and references to Appendices
MICMAC CAMP.	1/3/17		General work on C.T.s.	
	2/3/17		do	
	3/3/17		do	
	4/3/17		do	
	5/3/17		do	
	6/3/17		Rest day & bathing.	
	7/3/17		General work on C.T.s.	
	8/3/17		do	
	9/3/17		do	
	10/3/17		do	
	11/3/17		do	
	12/3/17		Rest day & bathing.	
	13/3/17		General work on C.T.s.	
	14/3/17		do	
	15/3/17		do	
	16/3/17		do	
	17/3/17		do	
	18/3/17		do	
	19/3/17		Rest day & bathing.	
	20/3/17		General work on C.T.s. Relieved of Ridge Wood Sector.	
	21/3/17		General work on C.T.s	
	22/3/17		do	
	23/3/17		do	
	24/3/17			
	25/3/17			

Army Form C. 2118.

WAR DIARY
or
INTELLIGENCE SUMMARY 19th Bn Middlesex Regt (Pioneers)
(Erase heading not required.)

Place	Date	Hour	Summary of Events and Information	Remarks and references to Appendices
Mericourt Camp	26/3/17		General work on C.T's.	
	27/3/17		Rest day & bathing.	
	28/3/17		General work on C.T's	
	29/3/17		do	
	30/3/17		do	
	31/3/17		do	

A. Moore. LT. COLONEL.
COMMANDING 19TH (S) BN.
MIDDLESEX REGT. (PIONEERS.)

WAR DIARY
or
INTELLIGENCE SUMMARY

(Erase heading not required.)

Army Form C. 2118.

1915 (9) B. Middlesex Bn (Pioneers)

WD /2

Place	Date	Hour	Summary of Events and Information	Remarks and references to Appendices
Micmac Camp	1/4/17		Work on C.T's.	
	2/4/17		do	
	3/4/17		Rest day & bathing	
	4/4/17		Work on CT's	
	5/4/17		do	
	6/4/17		do	
	7/4/17		do	
	8/4/17		do	
	9/4/17		do	
	10/4/17		Rest day & CT's	
	11/4/17		Work on CT's	
	12/4/17		do	
	13/4/17		do	
	14/4/17		do	
	15/4/17		do	
	16/4/17		do	
	17/4/17		Rest day & bathing.	
	18/4/17		Work on CT's	
	19/4/17		do	
	20/4/17		do	
	21/4/17		do	
	22/4/17		do	
	23/4/17		do	
	24/4/17		Rest day & bathing	
	25/4/17		Work on CT's	
	26/4/17		do	
	27/4/17		do	
	28/4/17		do	
	29/4/17		do	
	30/4/17		do	

J.J. Hume
LT. COLONEL
COMMANDING 19TH (S) BN.
MIDDLESEX REGT. (PIONEERS.)

From :- Officer Commanding
       19th (S) Battalion
       Middlesex Regt.(Pioneers.)

To   :- Headquarters,
        41st Division, A.

                    Herewith War Diary for month of

May, 1917.

                              A. Thoms   Lt. Col.
                          Commanding 19th (S) B'n
June 1st 1917.   Middlesex Regt.(Pioneers.)

No. 733.

Army Form C. 2118.

WAR DIARY
or
INTELLIGENCE SUMMARY

(Erase heading not required.)

17th (S/B Middlesex Regt (Pioneers)

19 — May 1917

Vol 13

Instructions regarding War Diaries and Intelligence Summaries are contained in F. S. Regs., Part II. and the Staff Manual respectively. Title Pages will be prepared in manuscript.

Place	Date	Hour	Summary of Events and Information	Remarks and references to Appendices
Mirvaux Camp	1/5/17		Rest day. Bathing.	
	2/5/17		Work all C.T.'s tramlines & road	
	3/5/17		do	
	4/5/17		do	
	5/5/17		do	
	6/5/17		do	
	7/5/17		do	
	8/5/17		Rest day. Bathing.	
	9/5/17		Work on C.T.'s, tramways & road	
	10/5/17		do	
	11/5/17		do	
	12/5/17		do	
	13/5/17		do	
	14/5/17		do	
	15/5/17		Rest day.	
	16/5/17		Work on C.T.'s, tramways & road	
	17/5/17		do	
	18/5/17		do	
	19/5/17		do	— 'B' Coy returned to duty with unit from Corps Light Rly.
	20/5/17		do	
	21/5/17		Rest day. Bathing.	
	22/5/17			

Army Form C. 2118.

WAR DIARY
or
INTELLIGENCE SUMMARY
(Erase heading not required.)

Instructions regarding War Diaries and Intelligence Summaries are contained in F. S. Regs., Part II. and the Staff Manual respectively. Title Pages will be prepared in manuscript.

Place	Date	Hour	Summary of Events and Information	Remarks and references to Appendices
Thiennes Camp	23/5/17		Work on CT's, roads & tramways.	
	24/5/17		do.	
	25/5/17		do.	
	26/5/17		do.	
	27/5/17		do.	
	28/5/17		do.	
	29/5/17		Rest Day.	
	30/5/17		Work on CT's, road & tramways.	
	31/5/17		do.	

A. Hamm
LT. COLONEL,
COMMANDING 19TH (S) BN.
MIDDLESEX REGT. (PIONEERS.)

From :- Officer Commanding
       19th (S) Battalion
       Middlesex Regt.(Pioneers.)

To   :- Headquarters,
        41st Division, A.

Herewith War Diary for the month of June 1917.

No. 789.

[signature] Major
for Lt. Col.
Commanding 19th (S) B'n
Middlesex Regt.(Pioneers.)

June 30th 1917.

Army Form C. 2118.

WAR DIARY
or
INTELLIGENCE SUMMARY
(Erase heading not required.)

19th (S) Bn Middlesex R/l (Pioneers)   Vol 14

Place	Date	Hour	Summary of Events and Information	Remarks and references to Appendices
Micmac Camp	1/6/17		Work on Road, tramways & C.T's	
	2/6/17		do	
	3/6/17		do	
	4/6/17		do	
	5/6/17		do	
	6/6/17		Bn moved up into front line previous to attack	
G.H.Q 2nd line	7/6/17		After infantry had captured the DAMMSTRASSE, A & B Coys across no-mans-land, C Coy on tramway & D Coy on ST ELOI – DAMMSTRASSE road.	
	8/6/17		A & D Coys road work. B & C Coys tramways.	
	9/6/17		do	
	10/6/17		do	
	11/6/17		do	
	12/6/17		do	
	13/6/17		do	
	14/6/17		do	
	15/6/17		do	
	16/6/17		Bn moved into camp at Sheet 27. N.30.b.5.	
VIERSTRAAT	17/6/17		A Coy on OBER AVENUE, B Coy on OBER AVENUE (S.I.), C Coys tramways, D Coy road.	
	18/6/17		do	
	19/6/17		Bn road party	
	20/6/17		Work on C.T., road & tramways.	
	21/6/17		do	
	22/6/17		do	
	23/6/17		do	
	24/6/17		do	
	25/6/17		do	
	26/6/17		Rectm Rest day & bathing.	

WAR DIARY
or
INTELLIGENCE SUMMARY

(Erase heading not required.) 19th (S) Bn Middlesex R[?] (Pioneers)

Army Form C. 2118.

Place	Date	Hour	Summary of Events and Information	Remarks and references to Appendices
VIERSTRAAT	27/6/17		Work on CTs, roads & tramways.	
	28/6/17		do	
	29/6/17		do	
	30/6/17		Handed over work to 11th Bn R. Welsh Fusiliers (Pioneers).	

A.J. Turner ma[?] Lt Col.
Comdg 19th (S) Bn Middlesex R[?] (Pioneers)

From :- Officer Commanding
        19th (S) Battalion
        Middlesex Regt.(Pioneers.)

To   :- Headquarters,
        41st Division, A.

        Herewith War Diary for the

month of JULY 1917.

No. 861.   A. Hours   Lt. Col.
                    Commanding 19th (S) B'n
                    Middlesex Regt.(Pioneers.)

August 1st 1917.

Army Form C. 2118.

WAR DIARY
or
INTELLIGENCE SUMMARY

(Erase heading not required.) 19th (S) Bn Middlesex Regt (Pioneers)

Vol. 15

Instructions regarding War Diaries and Intelligence Summaries are contained in F. S. Regs., Part II. and the Staff Manual respectively. Title Pages will be prepared in manuscript.

Place	Date	Hour	Summary of Events and Information	Remarks and references to Appendices
BERTHEN	1/7/17		Bn moved out to rest.	
	2/7/17		Rest	
	3/7/17		do	
	4/7/17		do	
	5/7/17		do	
	6/7/17		do	
	7/7/17		do	
	8/7/17		do. Batt'n inspected by G.O.C.	
	9/7/17		do.	
	10/7/17		do.	
MILLEKRUISSE	11/7/17		Bn moved to MILLEKRUISSE. Two Coys working under C.E. V Corps + two under C.R.E. 47th Division.	
	12/7/17		A Coy working on tracks, B+C roads, D gun positions.	
	13/7/17		do do do do	
	14/7/17		do do do do	
	15/7/17		do do do do	
	16/7/17		do do do do	
	17/7/17		(tramways) (roads) D gun positions	
	18/7/17		do do do do	
	19/7/17		do do do do	
	20/7/17		do do do do	
	21/7/17		do do do do	
	22/7/17		do do do do	
	23/7/17		do do — do do	
	24/7/17		do do do do	
	25/7/17		do do do do	
	26/7/17			
	27/7/17			
	28/7/17			
	29/7/17			

Army Form C. 2118.

WAR DIARY
or
INTELLIGENCE SUMMARY
(Erase heading not required.)

19th (S) Bn Middlesex Regt (Pioneers)

Place	Date	Hour	Summary of Events and Information	Remarks and references to Appendices
RIDGE WOOD	24/7/17		A Coy at OAF AVENUE B Coy OPTIC AVENUE 'E' Coy CHESTER RD- D Coy on tracks	
do	25/7/17		do do do do	
do	26/7/17		do do 'C' Coy tramways D Coy on transport tracks	
do	27/7/17		do do do do	
do	28/7/17		do do do do	
do	29/7/17		do do do do	
do	30/7/17		Rest day. Bn moved up to position Fools VIERSTRAAT - YPRES road.	
VIERSTRAAT	31/7/17		H.M Division attacked at 3.50 a.m. A Coy worked on OAF AVENUE, B Coy on OPTIC AVENUE, 'C' Coy on tramways, D Coy on transport tracks.	

A.V.Munro LT. COLONEL.
COMMANDING 19TH (S) BN
MIDDLESEX REGT. (PIONEERS)

From :- Officer Commanding
       19th (S) Battalion
       Middlesex Regt.(Pioneers.)

To :- Headquarters,
      41st Division, A.

Herewith War Diary for the

month of AUGUST 1917.

No. 916.   [signature] Lt. Col.
                        Commanding 19th (S) B'n
                        Middlesex Regt.(Pioneers.)

August 31st 1917.

Army Form C. 2118.

WAR DIARY
or
INTELLIGENCE SUMMARY
(Erase heading not required.)

Instructions regarding War Diaries and Intelligence Summaries are contained in F.S. Regs., Part II and the Staff Manual respectively. Title Pages will be prepared in manuscript.

19th (S) Bn Middlesex Regt (Pioneers)

Vol 16

Place	Date	Hour	Summary of Events and Information	Remarks and references to Appendices
VIERSTRAAT.	1/8/17		'A' Coy working on TAF AVENUE, 'B' Coy on OPTIC AVENUE, 'C' Coy on Tramlines, 'D' Coy on transport/trucks.	
do	2/8/17		do do do do	
do	3/8/17		do do do do	
do	4/8/17		do do do do	
do	5/8/17		do do do do	
do	6/8/17		do do do do	
do	7/8/17		do do do do	
do	8/8/17		do do do do	
do	9/8/17		do do do do	
do	10/8/17		do do do do	
do	11/8/17		do do Coys on tracks + tramlines. 'D' Coy working with 233rd Coy	
do	12/8/17		do do do do	
do	13/8/17		do do do do	
do	14/8/17		'A' Coy moved to BERTHEN. B & D rest.	
BERTHEN	15/8/17		H.Q, B & D moved to BERTHEN by bus.	
do	16/8/17		Cleaning up.	
do	17/8/17		G.O.C. inspected Battn.	
do	18/8/17		Army Comdr inspected Battn	
do	19/8/17		Church parades.	
STAPLE	20/8/17		Bn moved to STAPLE area by march route.	
ETREHEM	21/8/17		ETREHEM do do	
do	22/8/17		Rest.	
do	23/8/17		do.	

WAR DIARY
or
INTELLIGENCE SUMMARY

Army Form C. 2118.

19th Middlesex Regt (Pioneers)

Place	Date	Hour	Summary of Events and Information	Remarks and references to Appendices
ETREHEM	24/8/17		Division inspected by C in C.	
	25/8/17		Training	
	26/8/17		Church parades	
	27/8/17		Training	
	28/8/17		Training	
	29/8/17		Transport proceeded by road to MILLEKRUISSE.	
RIDGE WOOD	30/8/17		Bn moved by bus to RIDGE WOOD area.	
	31/8/17		A Coy assembly trenches, B & D Coys forward roads.	

D Maxwell Lt Colonel
COMMANDING 19TH (S) BN.
MIDDLESEX REGT. (PIONEERS.)

Army Form C. 2118.

WAR DIARY
or
INTELLIGENCE SUMMARY

(Erase heading not required.)

19th (S) Bn. Middlesbrough Regt (Pioneers)

Place	Date	Hour	Summary of Events and Information	Remarks and references to Appendices
RIDGE WOOD	1/9/17		A Coy Assembly Trenches. B C & D Coys forward roads.	16/17
	2/9/17		do do do	
	3/9/17		do do do	
	4/9/17		do do do	
	5/9/17		do do do	
	6/9/17		do do do	
	7/9/17		B Coy Duckboard Walk. C & D Coys forward roads.	
	8/9/17		A & B Coys Duckboard walk. C Coy do. D Coy do.	
	9/9/17		do do do do	
	10/9/17		do do do do	
	11/9/17		do do do do	
	12/9/17		do do do do	
	13/9/17		do do do do	
	14/9/17		do do do do	
	15/9/17		do do do do	
	16/9/17		do do do do	
	17/9/17		do do do do	
	18/9/17		do do do do	
	19/9/17		Bartin Park.	
	20/9/17		Division attacked at 5.40am. A & B Coys duckboard walk. C Coy tramway. D Coy mule track.	
	21/9/17		A & B Coys Duckboard walks. C Coy tramways. D Coy mule track.	
	22/9/17		do do do do	
	23/9/17		do do do do	
	24/9/17		Battn. standing by for orders.	

WAR DIARY
or
INTELLIGENCE SUMMARY

(Erase heading not required.)

Army Form C. 2118.

Place	Date	Hour	Summary of Events and Information	Remarks and references to Appendices
RIDGE WOOD	25/9/17	—	Battn. move to L'EGERREEST.	
L'EGERREEST	26/9/17	—	" " " LA PANNE.	
LA PANNE	27/9/17	—	" at Rest.	
"	28/9/17	—	" "	
"	29/9/17	—	" "	
"	30/9/17	—	" "	

A. Eborno
LT. COLONEL.
COMMANDING 19TH (S) BN
MIDDLESEX REGT. PIONEERS

From :- Officer Commanding
       19th (S) Battalion
       Middlesex Regt.(Pioneers).

To   :- 41st Division, A.

    Herewith War Diary for the
month of OCTOBER 1917.

No. 26.   Lieut.Colonel,
                        Commanding 19th (S) B'n
                        Middlesex Regt.(Pioneers).

November 1st 1917.

From:- Officer Commanding
19th (S) Bn. Middlesex Regt. (Pioneers).

To:- Headquarters,
41st Division, A.

Herewith War Diary for
the month of September, 1917.

A Hume Lt Col.
Cmdg 19th (S) Bn
No. 964. Middlesex Regt (Pioneers)

October 1st 1917.

Army Form C. 2118.

WAR DIARY
or
INTELLIGENCE SUMMARY
(Erase heading not required.)

1st/9th 1918. Winchester Rgt. (Queens)

Vol. 18

Instructions regarding War Diaries and Intelligence Summaries are contained in F. S. Regs., Part II. and the Staff Manual respectively. Title Pages will be prepared in manuscript.

Place	Date	Hour	Summary of Events and Information	Remarks and references to Appendices
LA PANNE	1/10/17		Training	
"	2/10/17		"	
"	3/10/17		"	
"	4/10/17		"	
"	5/10/17		"	
"	6/10/17		"	
"	7/10/17		"	
OOST DUNKERQUE BAINS	8/10/17		Battn. moved to OOST DUNKERQUE BAINS.	
"	9/10/17		A + B Coys 6T's. C Coy Tramways. D Coy moved.	
"	10/10/17		A Coy moved to LA PANNE, B Coy Dumps Nieuport, C Coy Supply Tramways, D Coy GT's.	
"	11/10/17		A Coy Wagon lines do	
"	12/10/17		do do do do	
"	13/10/17		do do do do	
"	14/10/17		do do do do	
"	15/10/17		do do do do	
"	16/10/17		do do do do	
"	17/10/17		do do do do	
"	18/10/17		do do do do	
"	19/10/17		do do do do	
"	20/10/17		do do do do	
"	21/10/17		do do do do	
"	22/10/17		do do do do	
"	23/10/17		do do do do	

WAR DIARY
or
INTELLIGENCE SUMMARY

Army Form C. 2118.

1 q 1t (W) Bn. M.G.C. — By/ (Pioneers)

Place	Date	Hour	Summary of Events and Information	Remarks and references to Appendices
OOST DUNKERKE BAINS	23/10/17		A Coy wagon lines at LA PANNE. B Coy under 1st & 2nd Div. C Coy. training. roads camps	B Coy. B.T.O. & 1st Div. Operations Orders
	24/10/17		do do do	do
	25/10/17		do do do	do
	26/10/17		do do do	do
	27/10/17		do do do	do
	28/10/17		do do do	do
COUDEKERQUE	29/10/17		Battn. move to COUDEKERQUE personnel by buses transport by roads.	
	30/10/17		Kit inspection making up deficiencies.	A. L. Lyons Lieut. Col.
	31/10/17		Inspections.	Comdg. 19th (W) Bn. M.G.C. (Pioneers)

Pioneers.
41st Div.

Battn. returned with
Div. from Italy
3/8.3.18.

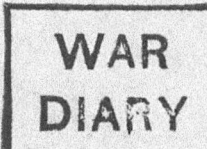

19th BATTN. THE MIDDLESEX REGIMENT.

M A R C H

1 9 1 8

Army Form C. 2118.

War Diary of Middlesex Regt. (Pioneers)

VOL 23

Instructions regarding War Diaries and Intelligence Summaries are contained in F. S. Regs., Part II. and the Staff Manual respectively. Title pages will be prepared in manuscript.

19TH (S) BATT.
MIDDLESEX REGT.
(PIONEERS)

From:- Officer Commanding
19th (S) Battalion
Middlesex Regt. (Pioneers.)

To :- G.O.C.,
" :- 2nd London Bde.

Period of March 1918.

A Villiers
Commanding 19th (S) Bn.
Middlesex Regt. (Pioneers.)

April 7th 1918.

Place	Date	Hour		Remarks and references to Appendices
Italy	1/3/18 and 2/3/18		Resting at	
Italy	3/3/18		Entrained	
France	4/3/18 to 8/3/18		Detrained	
COUTURELLE	9/3/18		Rest.	
do.	10/3/18 to 18/3/18		Training	
ARRAS	19/3/18		Marched to A.	
"	20/3/18		Working on A.	
"	21/3/18		"	
"	22/3/18		"	
BEUGNÂTRE	23/3/18		Marched to B. took over from 184th R.F.?	
"	24/3/18		Enemy attacks until comp. withdrawn, Batt. held on	
BIEFVILLERS LES-BAPAUME	25/3/18		Enemy attacking our right on the enemy Batt. in ?????	withdraw leaving heavy casualties PETIT
FONQUEVILLERS	26/3/18			

WAR DIARY
or
INTELLIGENCE SUMMARY

Army Form C. 2118.

19th (S) B. Middlesex Regt (Pioneers)

Vol 23

Place	Date	Hour	Summary of Events and Information	Remarks and references to Appendices
Italy	1/3/18 and 2/3/18		Resting at MONASTIERO.	
Italy	3/3/18 to 7/3/18		Entrained at FONTANAVIA (Italy).	
France	8/3/18		Detrained at MONDICOURT (France)	
COUTURELLE	9/3/18		Rest.	
do	10/3/18 15/3/18		Training	
ARRAS.	18/3/18		Marched to ARRAS.	
"	19/3/18		Working on the system of defence	
"	20/3/18		"	
"	21/3/18		"	
"	22/3/18		"	
BEUGNÂTRE	23/3/18		Marched to BIHUCOURT. Went in the line at night at BEUGNÂTRE.	
"	24/3/18		Enemy attacked our position at about 6pm. Units on flanks withdrew from 15th K.R.R. Battn held on until compelled to withdraw to BIEFVILLERS-LES-BAPAUME.	
BIEFVILLERS LES-BAPAUME	25/3/18		Enemy attacked our position in the morning. Troops on right flank withdrew leaving our right exposed. Battn held on to our position & inflicted heavy casualties on the enemy until compelled to withdraw to ACHIET-LE-PETIT.	
FONQUEVILLERS	26/3/18		Battn in reserve line.	

Army Form C. 2118.

WAR DIARY
or
INTELLIGENCE SUMMARY.
(Erase heading not required.)

19th(S) Bn. Middlesex R/ (Pioneers)

Place	Date	Hour	Summary of Events and Information	Remarks and references to Appendices
BIENVILLERS- AU-BOIS.	27/3/18		Rest.	
GOMMECOURT	28/3/18		Battn in Reserve Posn.	
ABLAINZEVELLE	29/3/18		Took over front line from 1/10th Manchester Regt at night.	
"	30/3/18		Held line. Enemy artillery rungs active.	
"	31/3/18		Enemy artillery m.gs - snipers active throughout the day. Relieved by 23rd Sx Middlesex Rgt at night & went into support.	

A. V. James
LT. COLONEL.
COMMANDING 19TH (S) BN.
MIDDLESEX REGT. (PIONEERS.)

41st Divisional Pioneers

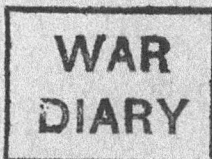

19th BATTALION

THE MIDDLESEX REGIMENT
Pioneers

APRIL 1918

From Officer Commanding
19th (S) Battalion
Middlesex Regt (Pioneers)

To D.A.G.
3rd Echelon, G.H.Q.

Herewith War Diary for

the month of April 1918.

[Signature] Lt. Colonel
Comdg 19th (S) Bn Middlesex
Regt (Pioneers)

A.2.

May 1st 1918

WAR DIARY or INTELLIGENCE SUMMARY

Army Form C. 2118.

19th (S.) Bn. Middlesex Regt (Pioneers)

Vol 24

Place	Date	Hour	Summary of Events and Information	Remarks and references to Appendices
Albouzeville	1/4/18		In line all day. Relieved by 5th Warwicks at night.	
Halloy	2/4/18		Marched to PAS in morning to HALLOY in afternoon.	
Beauvoir	3/4/18		Marched to BEAUVOIR.	
	4/4/18		Entrained at PREVENT.	
STEENVOORDE	5/4/18		Arrived at STEENVOORDE.	
	6/4/18		Rest	
	7/4/18		Rest	
	8/4/18		Rest	
LA BRIQUE	9/4/18		Moved by light Railway to LA BRIQUE, N. of YPRES.	
	10/4/18		Work on PASSCHENDAELE Sector	
	11/4/18		do	
	12/4/18		do	
YPRES	13/4/18		Bn moved into billets in YPRES.	
	14/4/18		do	
	15/4/18		do	
	16/4/18		do	
	17/4/18		do	

Army Form C. 2118.

WAR DIARY
or
INTELLIGENCE SUMMARY. 19th (S.)Bn Middlesex R. (Pioneers)
(Erase heading not required.)

Place	Date	Hour	Summary of Events and Information	Remarks and references to Appendices
YPRES.	17/4/18		Work on PASSCHENDAELE Sector (Army Battle Zone.)	
	18/4/18		do	
	19/4/18		do	
	20/4/18		do	
	21/4/18		Bn moved to GOLDFISH CHATEAU. Work chitte	
	22/4/18		Work on Army Battle Zone	
	23/4/18		do	
	24/4/18		do	
	25/4/18		do	
VLAMERTINGHE	26/4/18		Work on 1/3rd & 4th defenced areas.	
	27/4/18		Work on GREEN LINE. Moved into billets near this work	
	28/4/18		do	
	29/4/18		do	
	30/4/18		do	

LT. COLONEL
COMMANDING 19TH (S.) BN.
MIDDLESEX REGT. (PIONEERS.)

From :- Officer Commanding
       19th (S) Battalion
       Middlesex Regt.(Pioneers.)

To :- D.A.G.,
       3rd Echelon,
       Base.

　　　　　　　Herewith War Diary for the

month of MAY, 1918.

G.691.   Lt. Colonel,
                           Commanding 19th (S) B'n
                           Middlesex Regt.(Pioneers.)

May 31st 1918.

19M(S) Battn. MIDDLESEX REGT.

Army Form C. 2118.

WAR DIARY
or
INTELLIGENCE SUMMARY.
(Erase heading not required.)

Vol 25

19th(S) BATTALION,
MIDDLESEX REGT.
(PIONEERS).

Instructions regarding War Diaries and Intelligence Summaries are contained in F. S. Regs., Part II. and the Staff Manual respectively. Title pages will be prepared in manuscript.

Place	Date	Hour	Summary of Events and Information	Remarks and references to Appendices
VLAMERTINGHE	1/5/18		The Battalion employed on constructing the GREEN LINE.	
"	2/5/18		" " " " " " "	
"	3/5/18		'A' and 'B' Coy on GREEN LINE. 'C' Coy on tracks & roads.	
"	4/5/18		" " " " " " "	
"	5/5/18		Rest Day.	
"	6/5/18		'A' and 'B' Coy on GREEN LINE. 'C' Coy on tracks & roads.	
"	7/5/18		" " " " " " "	
"	8/5/18		" " " " " " "	
"	9/5/18		" " " " " " "	
"	10/5/18		" " " " " " "	
"	11/5/18		Rest for 'A' and 'B' Coys. 'C' Coy on tracks and roads.	
"	12/5/18		'A' & 'B' Coys work on C.T. in front of YPRES. C Coy on tracks & roads.	
"	13/5/18		" " " " " " "	
"	14/5/18		" " " " " " "	
"	15/5/18		" " " " " " "	
"	16/5/18		" " " " " " "	

WAR DIARY
or
INTELLIGENCE SUMMARY.

19th (S) Battn. Middlesex Regt.

Army Form C. 2118.

(Erase heading not required.)

19th (S) BATTALION,
MIDDLESEX REGT.
(PIONEERS).

Instructions regarding War Diaries and Intelligence Summaries are contained in F.S. Regs., Part II. and the Staff Manual respectively. Title pages will be prepared in manuscript.

Place	Date	Hour	Summary of Events and Information	Remarks and references to Appendices
Vlamertinghe	17/3/18		'A' & 'B' Coys working on R.E. in front of YPRES, 'C' Coy on Roads & tramways	
"	18/3/18		"	
"	19/3/18		"	
"	20/3/18		"	
"	21/3/18		"	
"	22/3/18		"	
"	23/3/18		"	
"	24/3/18		"	
"	25/3/18		"	
"	26/3/18		"	
"	27/3/18		"	
"	28/3/18		"	
"	29/3/18		"	
"	30/3/18		"	
"	31/3/18		"	

LT. COLONEL
COMMANDING 19TH (S) BN.
MIDDLESEX REGT. PIONEERS

From :- Officer Commanding
         19th (S) Battalion
         Middlesex Regt.(Pioneers.)

To :-   D. A. G.,
         3rd Echelon, Base.

            Herewith War Diary for the

month of JUNE 1918.

                                    Major

No. 765.   Lt. Colonel,
                         Commanding 19th (S) B'n
                         Middlesex Regt.(Pioneers.)

July 2nd 1918.

Army Form C. 2118.

WAR DIARY
or
INTELLIGENCE SUMMARY.
(Erase heading not required.)

19th C/B Middlesex by M Horton

Place	Date	Hour	Summary of Events and Information	Remarks and references to Appendices
YLAMERTYNGHE	June 1		Rest	Sht 26
ST JAN TER BIEZEN	2		Moved by light railway	
do	3		Rest	
BUYSSCHEURE	4th		Moved by train & march route	
	5th to 8th		Training	
EPERLECQUES	9th		Moved by march route	
	10th to 24th		Training	
BUYSSCHEURE	25th		Moved by march route	
ZERMEZEELE	26th		do. do.	
	27th to 29th		Training	
WIPPEN HOEK	30th		Moved by lorry & march route	

H. Ensor, Major
for LT. COLONEL.
COMMANDING 19TH (S) BN.
MIDDLESEX REGT. (PIONEERS.)

From: Officer Commanding
19th (S) B'n Middlesex Regt
(Pioneers).

486.

TO:- D.A.G.,
3rd Echelon, Base, France.

Herewith War Diary for
the month of July, 1918.

[signature]
Lt. Colonel,
Commanding 19th (S) B'n
Middlesex Regt (Pioneers)

August 1st, 1918.

Army Form C. 2118.

19th 'B' Middlesex Regt

WAR DIARY
or
INTELLIGENCE SUMMARY.
(Erase heading not required.)

Place	Date	Hour	Summary of Events and Information	Remarks and references to Appendices
WIPPEN HOEK	1/7/18		'A' & 'C' Coys work by night on C.T's. 'B' Coy on Div H.Q. Improvement of camp.	
"	2/7/18		"	
"	3/7/18		'B' Coy on Div H.Q. Improvement of camp.	
"	4/7/18		'B' Coy on screening of roads, Div H.Q. & camp. Supply party for H Coy	
"	5/7/18		'B' Coy	
"	6/7/18		"	
"	7/7/18		"	
"	8/7/18		"	
"	9/7/18		"	
"	10/7/18		"	
"	11/7/18		"	
"	12/7/18		"	
"	13/7/18		'A' 'B' & 'C' Coy on C.T's, roads & tracks.	
"	14/7/18		"	
"	15/7/18		"	
"	16/7/18		"	

19 "A" Bn. MIDDLESEX REGT.

Army Form C. 2118.

WAR DIARY
or
INTELLIGENCE SUMMARY.
(Erase heading not required.)

Instructions regarding War Diaries and Intelligence Summaries are contained in F. S. Regs., Part II. and the Staff Manual respectively. Title pages will be prepared in manuscript.

Place	Date	Hour	Summary of Events and Information	Remarks and references to Appendices
WIPPENHOEK	17/7/18		'A' 'B' & 'C' Coys on C.T's, roads & tracks.	
"	18/7/18		"	
"	19/7/18		"	
"	20/7/18		"	
"	21/7/18		" 'B' Coy reorganised.	
"	22/7/18		" 'A' & 'C' Coys move to HOOGGRAAF	
"	23/7/18		" 'A' & 'C' " at " by day	
"	24/7/18		"	
"	25/7/18		"	
"	26/7/18		"	
"	27/7/18		"	
"	28/7/18		"	
"	29/7/18		"	
"	30/7/18		"	
"	31/7/18		"	

Capt. & Hon. Capt.
(for) LT. COLONEL
COMMANDING 19TH (S) BN.
MIDDLESEX REGT. (PIONEERS)

Army Form C. 2118.

WAR DIARY
or
INTELLIGENCE SUMMARY.
(Erase heading not required.)

19/(D)B. Middlesex Regt (Pioneers)

Place	Date	Hour	Summary of Events and Information	Remarks and references to Appendices
WIPPENHOEK	August 16th		'A' & 'C' Coys HOOGGRAAF. Batt. working on C.T's & tracks.	
"	17		do.	
"	18		do. Coy Commandant reconnoitre covered C.T.s	
"	19		do. Batt. working on C.T's & tracks	
"	20/21/22		do. do.	
"	26		do. Commenced laying work on 2 new tramways Regt T.S.	
"	27		do. do.	
"	28		Work continued. Half transport moved to RENESCURE	
"	29		'B' & 'D' Coy's down. 'A' Coy from 4y 13rd to LUMINE	
ETREHEM	30		Battn. relieved by 9th Somerset Light Infantry and moved to TILQUES area	
"	31		Battn resting at ETREHEM	

19/(D)B. Middlesex
Regt (Pioneers)

Instructions regarding War Diaries and Intelligence Summaries are contained in F. S. Regs., Part II. and the Staff Manual respectively. Title pages will be prepared in manuscript.

P/4

Army Form C. 2118.

WAR DIARY

or ~~INTELLIGENCE SUMMARY.~~

19th Bn Middlesex Regt (Pioneers).

(Erase heading not required.)

27

Place	Date	Hour	Summary of Events and Information	Remarks and references to Appendices
	1916.			
ETREHEM	Apl 1st		Battalion resting. We receive orders to move by bus.	
HOOGRAAF [illegible]	2nd		Battalion embus [illegible] LEULINE and move to HOOGRAAF.	
	3rd		"B" & "C" Cos work on the HALLEBAST – VIERSTRAAT – BRASSERIE Road and	
			make a way through for timber. 5 casualties [illegible] by enemy on this road.	
	4th		A & C Cos move into huts behind OUDERDOM. Battn employed on all	
			roads East of LOCRE – HALLEBAST – OUDERDOM Road.	
	5th & 6th		Battn working on roads.	
	7th		— do — B Co move to huts behind OUDERDOM.	
	8th & 9th		— do —	
OUDERDOM [illegible]	10th		— do — Battn HQ move to farm behind OUDERDOM.	
	11th–12th			
	13th		A & B Cos work on C.Ts BOIS CARRE [illegible] & PERTH LANE [illegible]	
			C Coy on roads.	
	14th–17th		As above.	
	18th		All Coys work on [illegible]	
RENINGHELST [illegible]	19th		Work on roads. Bn HQ move to [illegible]	

To D.A.G.
3rd Echelon

OCT & NOV

Herewith War Diary
for Months of October &
~~November~~ 1918.

L. M. Dawson Major
Cdg 19(S)Bn Middlesex
Regt (Pioneers)

9/12/18.

Army Form C. 2118.

WAR DIARY
or
INTELLIGENCE SUMMARY.
(Erase heading not required.)

Instructions regarding War Diaries and Intelligence Summaries are contained in F. S. Regs., Part II. and the Staff Manual respectively. Title pages will be prepared in manuscript.

Place	Date	Hour	Summary of Events and Information	Remarks and references to Appendices
BEDFORD HOUSE YPRES	1-10-18		Batt'n. work on road from HOLLEBEKE CHATEAU to ZANDVOORDE	
"	2-10-18		Boys work on ST ELOI - HOLLEBEKE - HOLLEBEKE-CHATEAU - ZANDVOORDE ROAD	
	3rd		which was in a hopeless condition but made fit for traffic by noon	
			Boys work on ZANDVOORDE - GHELUVELT ROAD	
	5th		Troops as above, all boys billeted round about ZANDVOORDE	
HOOGE	6th		Boys rest. Battn. HQ moved to STERLING CASTLE	
"	8th & 9th		Boys work on BASSEVILLE - ZANDVOORDE avoiding ZANDVOORDE ROAD	
KLEIN ZILLEBEKE	10th		B. C. boys rest A boy work on BASSEVILLE - ZANDVOORDE ROAD	
"	11th		A & B boys ocean MENIN ROAD	
"	12th		B boy attached to the RFA for work on tracks	
"	13th		A & C boys rest - B with the RFA	
GHELUVE	14th, 15th		Division attack B boy make track for RFA. A & C boy work on roads in front of	
"			GHELUVE	
MOORSEELE	16th		Battn. move to MOORSEELE	
"	17th		All boys work on GHELUVE - DADIZEELE ROAD	
"	18th		Officers reconnoitre roads from MOORSEELE to COURTRAI	

Army Form C. 2118.

WAR DIARY
or
INTELLIGENCE SUMMARY.

(Erase heading not required.)

Instructions regarding War Diaries and Intelligence Summaries are contained in F. S. Regs., Part II, and the Staff Manual respectively. Title pages will be prepared in manuscript.

Place	Date	Hour	Summary of Events and Information	Remarks and references to Appendices
MOORSEELE	19th		Coys work on roads round DADIZEELE and MOORSEELE	
BISSEGHEM	20th		A & B Coys work on bridge over the LYS	
"	21st		B Coy reports to the R.F.A.	
"	22nd		A Coy not B Coy with RFA + B Coy work on road leading up to Bridgehead	
SWEYENGHEM	23rd		B Coy with RFA A Coy on the LE CHAT CABT. to KAPPELLE MILAE NE	
"	24th 25th		Road and C Coy on the SWEYENGHEM - KNOKKE ROAD.	
"	26th		B Coy with Artillery A. + b Coys work on the LE CHAT CABT. KAPPELLE	
			MILAENE ROAD	
MARCKE	27th		Battle goes out to rest	
"	28th		B + C Coys work on road near MARCKE - A Coy rest	
"	29th		Rest	
"	30th		Rest	
"	31st		Rest	

Lieut Col
Commanding 19437 Batt. Middlesex Regt.

From Officer Commanding
19th (S) Battn Middx Regt

To 41st Division A

MX709

Herewith original copy of War Diary for month ending Nov 30

[signature] Capt & Adj
for Lieut Colonel
Commanding 19th (S) Battn
Middlesex Regt (Pioneers)

30/11/17.

WAR DIARY or INTELLIGENCE SUMMARY.

Army Form C. 2118.

19th Bn Middlesex Regt (Pioneers)

Place	Date	Hour	Summary of Events and Information	Remarks and references to Appendices
MARCKE	1918 Nov 1		Battn. resting	
	2		Battn. marches to SWEVEGHEM	
SWEVEGHEM	3		" prepares for advance	
	4		" moves to INGOYGHEM	
INGOYGHEM	5		A. Coy carrying bridging material to R. SCHELDT	
	6,7,8		" " " "	
	9		Enemy retired. Battn. work on bridging R. SCHELDT & preparation of roads & Dr. tracks	
BERCHEM	10		BATTN. still employed bridging	
	11		CESSATION of HOSTILITIES work on ever 10"	
	12-13			
	14		march to OPBRAKEL	
OPBRAKEL	15-17		resting at OPBRAKEL	
	18		March to IDEGHEM	
IDEGHEM	19-30		REST & RECREATIONAL training. Alternate day parties out tracks	

Lt. Col. N...?
DO Cmdg 19th 19 Bn
Middlesex Regt

From :- Officer Commanding
19th Bn Middlesex
Regt. (Pioneers)

9

G1006

To :- D.A.G.
3rd Echelon
Base.

Herewith War Diary for the month of December 1918.

Major
Cdg. 19th Bn Middlesex
Regt. (Pioneers)

7th Jany 1919

Army Form C. 2118.

19 Middlesex

WAR DIARY
or
INTELLIGENCE SUMMARY.

(Erase heading not required.)

Instructions regarding War Diaries and Intelligence Summaries are contained in F. S. Regs., Part II. and the Staff Manual respectively. Title pages will be prepared in manuscript.

Place	Date DECEMBER	Hour	Summary of Events and Information	Remarks and references to Appendices
I DEGEM	1st to 9th		Resting at I.DEGEM	
"	10th		Inspected by G.O.C.	
"	11th		Presentation of French decorations by G.O.C. in square GRAMMONT	
ENGHIEN	12th		Marched to ENGHIEN	
HAL	13th		" " HAL	
BRAINE L'ALLEUD	14th		" " BRAINE L'ALLEUD	
"	15th, 16th		Resting	
MARBAISOUX	17th		Marched to MARBAISOUX	
SOMBREFFE	18th		" " SOMBREFFE	
DHUY	19th		" " DHUY	
FRANC-WARET	20th		" " FRANC-WARET	
BAS OHA	21st		" " BAS OHA	
"	22nd to 26th		Resting	
"	27th		Working on HUCCORGNE - BURDINNE ROAD.	
"	28th to 31st		" "	

Major
19th Middlesex
Regt (Service)

Army Form C. 2118.

WAR DIARY
or
INTELLIGENCE SUMMARY.
(Erase heading not required.)

19(D)Bn Middlesex Regt
(Pioneers)

Vol 33

Instructions regarding War Diaries and Intelligence Summaries are contained in F. S. Regs., Part II. and the Staff Manual respectively. Title pages will be prepared in manuscript.

Place	Date JANUARY 1919	Hour	Summary of Events and Information	Remarks and references to Appendices
BAS OHA	1st to 11th		Recreational & Educational Training. Also minor Road Repairs carried out.	
"	12th		Battalion entrained at HUY for GERMANY.	
UNTER-ESCHBACH	13th		Detrained at BENSBURG (COLOGNE AREA) and marched to billets at UNTER-ESCHBACH	
"	14th to 31st		Recreational & Educational Training. Guards on Bridges & important buildings, &c.	

February 5/1/1919

[signatures]
F.J Bland
Bay 19(S) Bn 76 Middx
Regt (Pioneers)

WAR DIARY
INTELLIGENCE SUMMARY
for February 1919

Army Form C. 2118.

(Erase heading not required.)

Place	Date	Hour	Summary of Events and Information	Remarks and references to Appendices
Hockkuch	1919 Feb 1		Battalion in same billets in Eschbach as from 13-1-1919.	
	12	10.00	Presentation of Colours by Army Commander. Battalion Parade. Address by Army Commander. History of the Battalion given by Lt Colonel A A Reid D.S.O. M.C. Fair weather.	
	13		Started woodcutting for pickets to wiring in connection with Divisional Defence scheme. Books 6 pictures 6 pictorial knicknacks.	
	17		Guards at HEUMAR and HEIDELBURGER STRASSE COLOGNE and also Guard attached to A.P.M. COLOGNE relieved. Work as usual.	
	19	9.30	Church Parade. Football match in the afternoon.	
	21		Lecture by Lt Young on "France and the French People"	
	22		Snowfall a foot. No work possible. Companies doing work parties.	
	25		Divisional Defence scheme received. Battalion allotted sector of hill. Brigade left sector in Manoeuvre of Resistance.	
	28		Lecture in the attack and defence by Army Chaplain.	

F Mark Capt A/Adj
for Lt Colonel
Commanding 19 (S) Battalion
Middlesex Regiment (Alderm)

Army Form C. 2118.

WAR DIARY
for March 1919
INTELLIGENCE SUMMARY
(Erase heading not required.)

19th Batt. Middlesex Regiment (Pioneers)

M 35

Place	Date 1919	Hour	Summary of Events and Information	Remarks and references to Appendices
UNTER ESCHBACH GERMANY	March 1-2		Companies cutting sticks in vicinity of ESCHBACH	
	2	09.45	Church Parade in A Company's Dining Hall	
	3		A and B Companies proceed to billet at LINDE. Companies employed in cutting fascines and improving the Living Road etc in accordance with Divisional Defence Scheme.	
	4		C Company proceeded to billet at WARTH and BLINDENDATE to be attached to 122 Coy R.E.	
	4-10		A and B the Company is being employed in cutting sticks for the Engineers. Work as usual	
	10		Divisional Cinema opened at ESCHBACH showing nightly	
	12		Commanding Officer - Lt Col H A Reid DSO, MC left to take up appointment as A/CRE London Division.	
	14		Lecture was given by Mr J.C. BEE-MASON in the Cinema Hall ESCHBACH on The Craft of the Bee-hunter.	
	18	9.30	New Draft of 4 Officers 117 Other Ranks from 13th Batt. Middlesex Regiment arrived for inspection.	
			Work as usual at LINDE and WARTH	
	19		100 Other Ranks are out for Trip on Rhine starting from BONN	
	19-22		Work as usual	

Sheet 2

Army Form C. 2118.

WAR DIARY
for March 1919
INTELLIGENCE SUMMARY
19th Battn Middlesex Regiment (Pioneers)

(Erase heading not required.)

Instructions regarding War Diaries and Intelligence Summaries are contained in F. S. Regs., Part II. and the Staff Manual respectively. Title pages will be prepared in manuscript.

Place	Date 1919	Hour	Summary of Events and Information	Remarks and references to Appendices
UNTER ISCHBACH GERMANY	March 22		New Draft absorbed into Companies. Appointments. Corporal C Pope 2 Richards. O/c B Coy. Lieut C C Baker O/c Headquarters Coy. Lieut C P Ball to A Coy. Lieut F W Davies Transport Officer	
	23		Work as usual. 2/Lieut W P Stewart reported from 13th Battn Middlesex Regt & was posted to C Company. Battalion Defence Scheme prepared & Scheme and forwarded to all Companies	
	24-31			
	31		5 Officers and 120 Other Ranks demobilysed. First Edition "Cologne Post" arrived	

T.G. Mackay-Lewis Major
Commanding 19/D Battalion
th Middlesex Regiment (Pioneers)

Army Form C. 2118.

WAR DIARY
for Month of April 1919.
INTELLIGENCE SUMMARY.
(Erase heading not required.)

Instructions regarding War Diaries and Intelligence Summaries are contained in F. S. Regs., Part II. and the Staff Manual respectively. Title pages will be prepared in manuscript.

Place	Date 1919	Hour	Summary of Events and Information	Remarks and references to Appendices
UNTER ESCHBACH	April 1-7		Companies at Linde at work on line of Road. Race to be for London Division Cup & Silver Cup.	
	8		52nd Battalion Middlesex Regiment consisting of Lt Col M B Burnard and 36 Officers arrived and Billeted (Beiotery) takeover strength of 19th Middlesex from Hy	
	10		Lt Col A.A Reid D.S.O, M.C. left for Battalion for Denbury.	
	14		Lt Col M B Burnard proceeded to England	
	8-16		Companies at Linde at work as usual	
	17		100 Other Ranks attended Concert at Y.M.C.A Kalk	
	22		Hrs. Hallion moved from Villa in Bensberg and camp pitched in Eschbach	
	24		Party 1 Officer and 40 Other Ranks made Route March to Refrath Rhine	
	26		Party of 4 Officers and 100 Other Ranks made Route to Khine	
	29		200 Other Ranks attended Reserved Race meeting at Kalk	
	29		200 Other Ranks attended Reserved Race meeting at Kalk	
	30		Football Match "Veterans versus Young Soldiers"	
	4-30		Hdqrs Company at work on Knoecaine	
	7-30		Companies at work as usual	

F.H. Hoffman
Commanding 19/5 Bn
Middlesex Regt.

London Duncan A. 19th (S.) Bn. Middlesex Regt. (Pioneers).

A 354

Army Form C. 2118.

WAR DIARY
or
~~INTELLIGENCE SUMMARY~~

(Erase heading not required.)

Instructions regarding War Diaries and Intelligence Summaries are contained in F. S. Regs., Part II. and the Staff Manual respectively. Title pages will be prepared in manuscript.

Place	Date	Hour	Summary of Events and Information	Remarks and references to Appendices
Unter-Eschbach Germany	1/5/19		Lieut. J. McDonald proceeded to HAVRE for duty with Base Commandant, HAVRE.	
ditto	2/5/19		German Labour Day. Procession passed through Batn. area. There were no civil disturbances.	
ditto	3/5/19		Lieut. L. M. Baker and 12 O. Ranks left for demobilisation.	
ditto	6/5/19		52 O.R. left for demobilisation.	
ditto			6 Officers and 200 O. Ranks proceeded to MULHEIM for attachment to VI th Corps Bridging Party.	
ditto	8/5/19		Lieut-Colonel W. T. Webb-Bowen, D.S.O. reported for duty as Commanding Officer	
ditto	9/5/19		Lieut. O. P. Atkinson, M.G. cross-posted to 19 th Middx Regt. from 4 th Middlesex	
ditto	10/5/19		11 Other ranks left for demobilisation.	
ditto	14/5/19		Commanding Officer held an inspection of H.Q. Coy Eschbach	
ditto	16/5/19		Alkehera Day. Battn. Sports held in afternoon. 2/Lieut R. H. Brown and 10 O.R. left for demobilisation.	
—	22/5/19		"E" Coy moved from BLINDENAAF to BENSBERG.	
—	23/5/19		"A" and "B" Coys. concentrated at ESCHBACH on being recalled from LINDE.	
U-Eschbach	28/5/19		Major L. H. Dawson and 4 other ranks left for demobilisation. 2/Lieuts. A. A. Fitzgerald and E. Burtlett cross-posted to 11 th Bn. The Queens (R.W.S.) Regt., ENGELSKIRCHEN.	
ditto	30/5/19		8 Other Ranks left for demobilisation.	

W. T. Webb-Bowen Lt Colonel
COMMANDING 19TH (S) BN.
MIDDLESEX REGT. (PIONEERS)

Army Form C. 2118.

WAR DIARY
INTELLIGENCE SUMMARY
(Erase heading not required.)

June, 1919.

Instructions regarding War Diaries and Intelligence Summaries are contained in F. S. Regs., Part II. and the Staff Manual respectively. Title pages will be prepared in manuscript.

Place	Date	Hour	Summary of Events and Information	Remarks and references to Appendices
	JUNE			
Unter-Eschbach	3rd	—	King's Birthday. Ceremonial parade in the morning. Holiday observed in the afternoon.	
do.	4th noon	—	Lieuts. E. F. Hrohn and A.V. Justice left for demobilization.	
do.	4th	—	2/Lt. F. Dews, Transport Officer, admitted 139 Field Ambulance, with diphtheria.	
	8th		Lieut. A. S. Bennett took over his duties.	
	—		Battalion Orderly Room, Band & "B" Coy moved from UNTER-ESCHBACH to IMMEKEPPEL.	
			(NOTE: During week ending 7/6/19. Baseball was introduced into the Batt. by Sports Officer)	
Immekeppel	9th		Whit-Monday. There was no training this day.	
do.	14th		2/Lieut. F. Dews, Transport Officer, discharged from Hospital & resumed duties.	
do.	14th		All blankets withdrawn from men except one per man.	
do.	18th	09.15	Route march in morning. H.Q., "A" & "B" Coys. were on parade.	
do.	19th		Major D. E. Owen, D.S.O., reported for duty as 2nd-in-command.	
do.	20-24		Awaiting orders for forward move into Germany.	
U-Eschbach	28		Major-Gen. Sir S.T.B. Lawford, K.C.B., G.O.C. London Division inspected Battn. at U-Eschbach (H.Q. "A" & "B" Coys) at 09.15. Inspected "C" Coy at BENSBERG at 10.00.	
			Capt. A. Twees, R.A.M.C., reported for duty as Medical Officer. Peace signed to-day.	
	30		"F" Coy (Bridging) moved from MULHEIM to IMMEKEPPEL & re-named "A" Coy. Previous "A" Coy.	Personnel posted to H.Q.; "B" & "C" Coys. "B" Coy. moved from IMMEKEPPEL to HONRATH to relieve 228 Coy, R.E.

MacKuller
COMMANDING 19TH (S) BN.
MIDDLESEX REGT. (PIONEERS.)

WAR DIARY

INTELLIGENCE SUMMARY

JULY, 1919.

Army Form C. 2118.

(Erase heading not required.)

Instructions regarding War Diaries and Intelligence Summaries are contained in F.S. Regs., Part II. and the Staff Manual respectively. Title pages will be prepared in manuscript.

Place	Date	Hour	Summary of Events and Information	Remarks and references to Appendices
IMMEKEPPEL	JULY 1919, 3rd	—	Capt. A. FUOSS, R.A.M.C. (Bn. Medical Officer) left Batt. on rejoining unit in IX Corps.	
UNTER-ESCHBACH	10th	—	Battalion Sports held in afternoon.	
IMMEKEPPEL	13th	—	Lieut. & Q.Mr. H. SOLLY proceeded to Rhine Army Reception Camp, COLOGNE, to join Pool of Quartermasters.	
do.	14th	—	Lieut. E.G. BAKER took over duties of /Adjutant, vice A/Capt. F.G. BLACK.	
do.	25th	—	"A" Coy. moved from IMMEKEPPEL to CÖLN-VINGST.	
do.	27th	—	"C" Coy. " " BENSBERG " UNTER-ESCHBACH.	
UNTER-ESCHBACH	28th 29th	—	Battalion Rifle Competition held.	
IMMEKEPPEL	30th	—	Capt. L. Bain, M.C. left for demobilization	
do.	31st	—	"B" Coy. moved from HONRATH to IMMEKEPPEL.	

W. J. West Sower
LT. COLONEL.
COMMANDING 19TH (S) BN.
MIDDLESEX REGT. (PIONEERS.)

19th (S.) Bn. Middlesex Regt. (Pioneers) August, 1919

Army Form C. 2118.

WAR DIARY or INTELLIGENCE SUMMARY.

(Erase heading not required.)

Place	Date	Hour	Summary of Events and Information	Remarks and references to Appendices
	August		Preliminary Remarks. During August the greater part of the Battalion was concentrated at UNTER-ESCHBACH and IMMEKEPPEL underwent as follows:— H.Q. Coy and "C" Coy at UNTER-ESCHBACH; Battn. H.Q. and "B" Coy at IMMEKEPPEL. No pioneer work was done by these Coys, the men undergoing training in drill, musketry and ordinary Infantry duties. Up to the 26th August, "A" Coy was detached at COLN-VINGST engaged on the construction of a Race Course Stand. The attitude of the German civilian population during the month was not markedly hostile, and no disturbances occurred in the unit's area.	
IMMEKEPPEL	4th		General Athletic Inter-Coy Football matches held.	
do.	11th		Lieuts. F.G. BLACK & G.V. Stanfford proceeded to NOYELLES, France, for duty with Chinese Labour Corps.	
	26th-30th		London Divisional Rifle Meeting held at EHRESHOVEN. The Divisional Cup was won by the unit for highest score.	
	27th		"A" Coy moved from COLN-VINGST to UNTER-ESCHBACH Coy., and recommenced Infantry Training.	

W.S. Webb-Bowen
LT COLONEL.
COMMANDING 19TH (S) BN.
MIDDLESEX REGT. (PIONEERS)

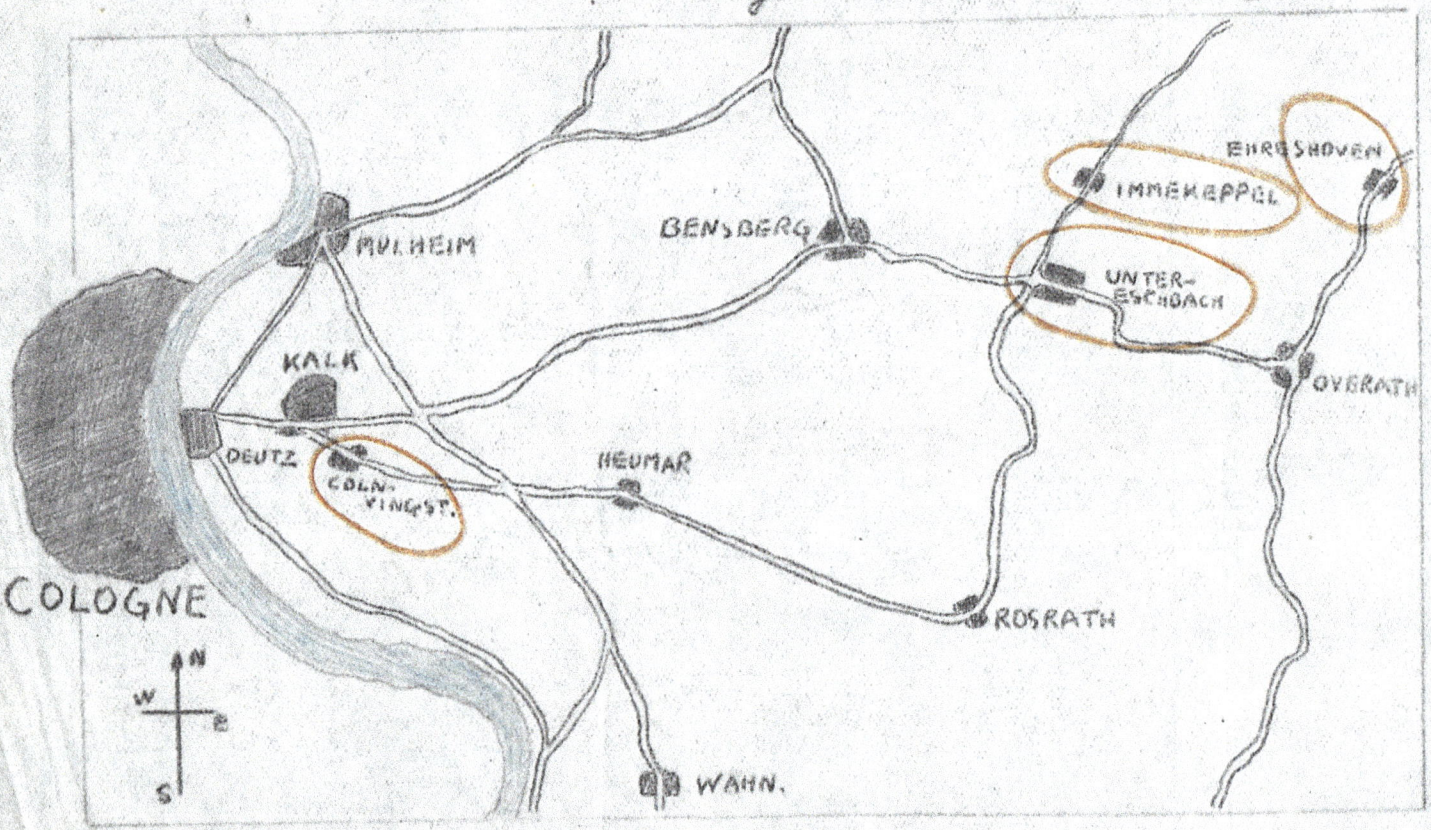

Headquarters "A"
19th (S.) Bn. MIDDLESEX REGT. (PIONEERS).
London Division

WAR DIARY
or
INTELLIGENCE SUMMARY.
(Erase heading not required.)

SEPTEMBER 1919.

Army Form C. 2118.

19TH (S) BN. MIDDLESEX REGT. (PIONEERS)
No. 10/1/10
Date 1/6/19

Instructions regarding War Diaries and Intelligence Summaries are contained in F. S. Regs., Part II. and the Staff Manual respectively. Title pages will be prepared in manuscript.

Place	Date	Hour	Summary of Events and Information	Remarks and references to Appendices
UNTER-ESCHBACH	Sept. 1st	0730	Battalion moved by march-route from UNTER-ESCHBACH to No.2 (P. of W.)CAMP, WAHN. Route taken as follows:- CROSS-ROADS, UNTER-ESCHBACH-HOFFNUNGSTHAL-VOLBERG-VIERKOTTEN-ROSRATH Road; thence S.W.by a track through KONIGSFORST FOREST (via the GEISTERBUSCH and KIELSHEIDE) to main URBACH-ALTENRATH Road, whence the ELSDORFER WEG was followed, leading direct to the Camp. Head of Column reached Camp at 10.00 hours. Stores were moved by lorries, which took the traffic route - CROSS-ROADS, UNTER-ESCHBACH - BENSBERG - IUSTHEIDE - BRÜCK - HOHENBERG - OSTHEIM - EIL - URBACH - WAHN. The Hutments taken over were in a very satisfactory condition, and comfortable quarters were established for all ranks. The Camp was a section of a large Camp used by the Germans during the war to house the prisoners employed on the Artillery Range, Ammunition Dumps, and Shell-Testing Laboratories, at WAHN. Capt.E.J.Lacey, R.A.M.C. assumed duties of Medical Officer 4/o Battalion.	See Sketch Map appended.
	do. 14th		The Battalion moved from No.2 (P. of W.) Camp to WAHN BARRACKS. The move commenced at 09.00 hours and was completed by 18.00 hours.	
	16th		Lieut.A.A.Woodland & 2/Lt.W.G.Lock transferred to England for demobilisation.	
	21st		Capt.B.G.Vaughan-Williams evacuated to England, "sick." Lieut.W.E.Reed transferred to England for demobilisation.	
	27th		All leave and demobilisation (except urgent compassionate cases) suspended, owing to outbreak of General Railway Strike in England.	
			REMARKS. During the month many men, previously attached to the London Divisional Field Coy., R.E., and London Div. M.T. Coy. and Military Police, Rhine Army, &c. were transferred to those units. This, and the demobilisation of 1916 volunteers and men who originally enlisted under the "Derby Scheme," brought down the strength of the Battalion from 43 Officers, 1100 Other Ranks, to 34 Officers, 714 Other Ranks. Many Guards were furnished by the unit during the month - notably the Guard at the LIND DYNAMITE FACTORY (Mr.WAHN), Camp Commandant's Guard, WAHN, and the WAHN AMMUNITION DUMP GUARD. Training was carried out on Infantry Lines during September 1919.	

Wahn, Germany.
1.10.1919.

D J Webb-Bowen Lt.-Colonel,
Commanding 19th (S.) Bn. Middlesex Regt. (Pioneers).

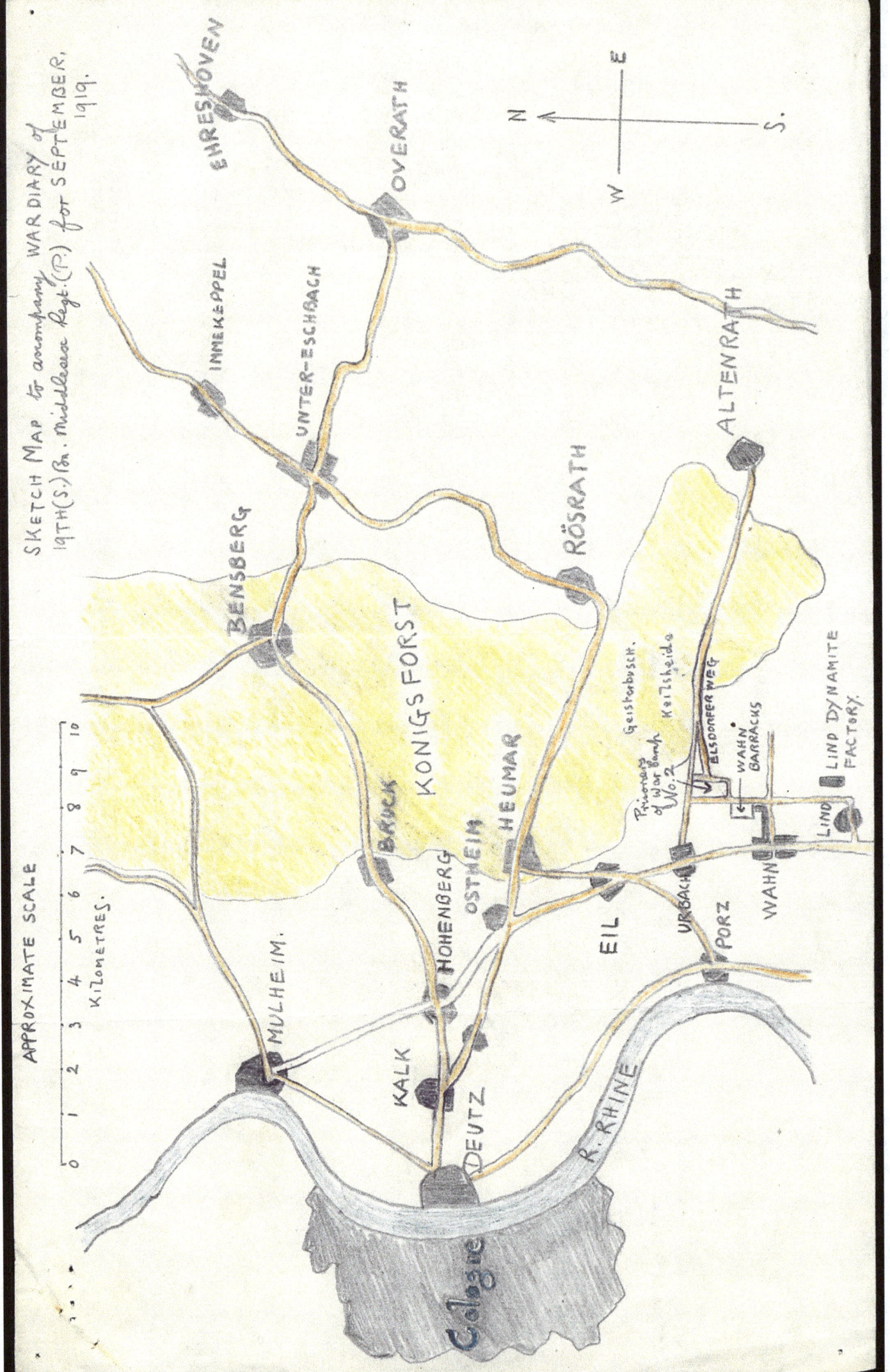

Headquarters, "A" 19th (S.) Bn. Middlesex Regt. (P)
London Division
Army Form C. 2118.

WAR DIARY
or
INTELLIGENCE SUMMARY.
(Erase heading not required.)

Instructions regarding War Diaries and Intelligence Summaries are contained in F. S. Regs. Part II. and the Staff Manual respectively. Title pages will be prepared in manuscript.

OCTOBER, 1919.
LONDON DIVISION,
RHINE ARMY.

Place	Date	Hour	Summary of Events and Information	Remarks and references to Appendices
WAHN BARRACKS	2nd		London Division "Q" Branch Disinfecting Scheme commenced in this unit. By this means all N.B.Os. and men were bathed and blankets, kit-bags and S.D. clothing of the whole Battalion were deloused in 2 consecutive days.	
do.	6th		Orders received unit to move to BRÜHL and be attached to NORTHERN DIVISION for tactical purposes.	
do.	10th		Advance party moved to BRÜHL by lorry.	
do.	12th		Battn. moved to BRÜHL by lorry to take over billets of 53rd Northumberland Fusiliers. Route:– WAHN – URBACH – EIL / KALK / DEUTZ – SUSPENSION BRIDGE – MARIENBURG – MESCHENICH – BRÜHL. BRÜHL the a town of about 19,000 inhabitants S. of COLOGNE on left bank of the Rhine. H.Q. Bn. and "B" Coy. were quartered in the SCHLOSS; "A" and "C" Coys in the ALUMAT HOSPITAL. The town was given a bad reputation for brawls by units previously quartered. No disturbances occurred during this unit's occupation.	
BRÜHL	20-31		Re-organization of Rhine Army. This unit selected for retention with the Rhine garrison force. All men (other than volunteers for Armies of Occupation) of age despatched to 23rd Middx Regt. shortly to depart for U.K. 70 men were this sent. 500 men and 13 officers were posted to this unit from the 7th and 23rd Battalions Middlesex Regt. This raised the strength of the Battn. again to slightly over 1,000 officers and men.	
BRÜHL	31st		Battn. moved N. by march route to BONNERSTRASSE BARRACKS, MARIENBURG. These Barracks were formerly the German Foot-Artillery Barracks. MARIENBURG is the most southerly suburb of COLOGNE, and is a well-to-do residential district.	

W. J. D Powe
Lt.-Colonel.
Comdg. 19th (S.) Bn. Middlesex Regt. (Pioneers).

www.ingramcontent.com/pod-product-compliance
Lightning Source LLC
Chambersburg PA
CBHW081543160426
43191CB00011B/1824